On the Future of Art

Essays by Arnold J. Toynbee, Louis I. Kahn,

Annette Michelson, B. F. Skinner, James Seawright,

J. W. Burnham, and Herbert Marcuse

Introduction by Edward F. Fry

Sponsored by The Solomon R. Guggenheim Museum

NEW YORK | THE VIKING PRESS

D1248803

Contents

Introduction *by Edward F. Fry*
· *vii* ·

Art: Communicative or Esoteric? *by Arnold J. Toynbee*
· *3* ·

Architecture: Silence and Light *by Louis I. Kahn*
· *21* ·

Art and the Structuralist Perspective *by Annette Michelson*
· *37* ·

Creating the Creative Artist *by B. F. Skinner*
· *61* ·

Phenomenal Art: Form, Idea, and Technique
by James Seawright
· *77* ·

The Aesthetics of Intelligent Systems *by J. W. Burnham*
· *95* ·

Art as a Form of Reality *by Herbert Marcuse*
· *123* ·

Introduction

Even before the end of the 1960s, it was apparent that the normally endemic crisis within contemporary art had reached an acute and problematic stage beyond all previous dimensions. Critical issues, which had long remained dormant and only partially resolved, emerged with a new urgency, and the very worth and function of art itself within society were being questioned by artists themselves as well as by critics.

In view of this situation, the Solomon R. Guggenheim Museum presented during 1969 a series of lectures on the general subject of the future of art, of which the essays printed herein are the consequence. Because the nature of the problem demanded fresh insights beyond the normal limits of critical and art-historical discourse, the participants were drawn in large part from areas not usually associated with contemporary art, ranging from the philosophy of history to psychology and social theory. The result, it is hoped, has been to situate the phenomenon of contemporary art in a larger context than is normally encountered.

Two practicing artists included in this group stand at almost opposite poles from each other: one, Louis Kahn, is considered by many to be the greatest living architect; the other, James Seawright, is a young sculptor who uses sophisticated electronics. Both, however, provide direct insight into the point of junction between theory and practice, as seen from two extremes of contemporary art.

The most general view taken is that of Toynbee, who here, as in his other writings, addresses himself to those over-all principles which can be shown to be operative descriptions of historical processes. By contrast, Professor Skinner and Miss Michelson both offer nonhistorical approaches to art. Skinner proposes that the problematic situation of contemporary art be analyzed from the viewpoint of the psychology of learning, a field in which he is an acknowledged pioneer. Miss Michelson's contribution is similarly an attempt to bring a nonaesthetic discipline to bear upon artistic problems, namely the structuralist analysis developed by the French anthropologist Lévi-Strauss.

The two most radical approaches in this collection are those of Mr. Burnham and Professor Marcuse. Both begin with the more or less explicit judgment that virtually all current art is compromised not only by its own hermetically self-generating aesthetics but also by the isolation of art from the major intellectual and social realities of our time. Burnham explores the researches in artificial intelligence, cybernetics, and systems, and relates them to the small number of artists thus far who have acknowledged these advances in their work. Marcuse, from his position as an eminent dialectician in the Marxist tradition of social philosophy, offers a compelling analysis and portrayal of the fallacies underlying the very concept of the "fine arts" in the modern world.

These selected points of view, while far from representing an exhaustive analysis of the situation of contemporary art, nevertheless pose many of the fundamental issues relevant to the problem of a future for art. It is a question that can be seen as part of an emerging concern of the culture as a whole with its own future, a tendency which has appeared rarely if ever before with its present intensity. Such a preoccupation, the newly born art or science of futurology, should be considered a symptom of an expansion, or perhaps even a mutation, of consciousness within the human species.

Edward F. Fry
Associate Curator
The Solomon R. Guggenheim Museum

New York
December 1969

On the Future of Art

Art: Communicative
or Esoteric?

ARNOLD J. TOYNBEE

Professor Toynbee, former Director of Studies at the Royal Institute of International Affairs and Professor Emeritus of the University of London, is the author of many important books on international history, including the many-volumed work A Study of History.

Should the artist work primarily for the community or primarily for himself? There is at least one other alternative: he may work for a coterie, within his community, that shares the artist's feelings, thoughts, and general outlook on life with the artist but not with the majority of the community of which the artist and his cronies are members. Which of these alternatives is the best is evidently an open question. Communities dislike dissent and innovation, and they have often tried to repress these by persecution. Yet changes, for better or for worse, in the ways of life of communities have usually been brought about, not by spontaneous simultaneous changes of heart and mind, but by a lead given by individuals or by minority groups—a lead that the majority may or may not follow, but that in any case it will seldom either accept or reject without debate that frequently boils over into strife.

If we believe—but this, too, is an open question—that, on the whole, mankind has progressed spiritually as well as materially within the relatively short span of recorded human history, then we shall be wary of endorsing the community's

3

instinctive condemnation of the heretic; and the heretic's pas-
sionate desire to convert his fellows, which, in the majority's
eyes, is his unforgivable offense, will seem to us to be his re-
deeming merit. It will seem to be meritorious because the would-
be missionary, however unwelcome initially or permanently, is
behaving socially. He is not seeking to keep his new knowledge or insight or power as a private preserve for himself or
for an inner circle of his cronies; he is seeking to make it common property. The founders of the historic higher religions
and their followers have been wholehearted missionaries. They
have believed that the new light which they have seen is of such
immense value to all mankind that it is their bounden duty to
try to spread it. Their missionary zeal has drawn persecution upon them at the start, but it has often won veneration
for them in the sequel. The descendants of the prophets' slay-
ers build the prophets' sepulchers.

The reason why importunate missionaries have come to be
venerated is that man is a social creature. His sociality is one
of the indispensable conditions for his survival. In isolation, a
human being is more helpless than many nonhuman species.
Robinson Crusoe became aware of his impotence when he
was marooned on his desert island. Yet Crusoe was not truly
isolated; for he managed to salvage and utilize a large part
of his wrecked ship's stores; and these stores were the product of the cooperative work of an elaborately organized society.

Crusoe was in, so to speak, posthumous communication with
the makers of these salvaged stores, and this just enabled him
to survive. Communion, direct or indirect, is the necessary condition for leading a social life. But there can be no communion
without means of communication, and social animals need the
greatest possible number, variety, and range of means of communication with each other. If man is right in holding that he
is the "highest" form of social animal that has made its appearance on this planet so far, his pretension is justified by the
superiority of his means of communication. In these he sur-
passes even the social insects, so far as we know.

Mankind's earliest means of communication was probably extrasensory perception—a faculty that was, and still is, shared by man with many other species. Though most people may not be aware of this, and many are reluctant to recognize it, it is probable that, when human beings talk to each other either individually or collectively, a good deal more passes between them than is conveyed by the words that are spoken and heard. Though all surviving human communities possess the gift of speech, language is probably a latecomer in the constantly increasing repertory of man's means of communication; and though, in the social intercourse between human beings, language has now pushed extrasensory perception out of its original central position into the fringe, we should be likely to find ourselves at a loss if this now ignored primitive means of communication were to be atrophied.

We have no means of knowing whether articulate human speech is older or younger than the earliest surviving specimens of visual art—the Upper Paleolithic cave paintings—but we do know that these paintings are older, by perhaps as much as twenty-five thousand years, than the earliest scripts in which the sounds of human speech were represented visually; so, in the realm of visual means of communication, painting, clay-modeling, scratching outlines on rocks, and even sculpture in the round had a long-lasting initial monopoly.

We know by experience that the gift for artistic creativity in all kinds of media differs greatly as between one person and another; so primitive works of art, like sophisticated works, are likely to have been made by specially gifted individuals; but we can also infer, from our acquaintance with relatively primitive societies which still survive, that primitive artists were not inhibited by their gift from remaining in full communion with the other members of their community. They did not feel that they were segregated from their fellows by their possession of a peculiar insight or faculty and that they could not re-enter into full communion unless they succeeded in converting their neighbors to their own way of feeling, thinking, and acting. They were not conscious of being specialists or experts or professionals, and, if they had been, this would not have given them a self-complacent sense of superiority; it would have made them diffident and unhappy, because it would have made them feel themselves to be isolated.

Primitive artists were not working for fellow artists, and, *a fortiori,* not for their own individual satisfaction. They were working for a community from which they themselves were not aloof. At this early stage in the history of means of communication there was no conscious distinction or contrast or opposition between artists and their public. This is shown by the fact that it did not occur to primitive artists to mark their works with a monogram or a signature in order to identify themselves as being the authors. They were doing their work on the community's behalf as its anonymous representatives. They could be content to remain anonymous because their representativeness was authentic.

Communication, of which the primitive artists were the agents, may have one or the other of two purposes, both of which are communal objectives, or it may have both purposes at once. The primary purpose of communication is operational: to produce a practical effect. The secondary purpose is instructional: to convey information. Of course these two purposes overlap. The conveyance of information may be necessary for taking action if the action is to be collective. Conversely, communication designed for producing some practical effect may incidentally convey information. Still, the distinction between operational and informational communicative art is valid and useful, as can be shown by giving some illustrations of each of the two varieties.

When we gaze at the pictures of animals and human beings in Upper Paleolithic cave paintings, we can only guess at their purpose. Presumably the painter had no need to explain the purpose to the other members of his community. They were as well aware of the purpose as he was himself. Moreover, if he had wanted to give an explanation, he could have done this only in fleeting gestures or words; he had no means of making a permanent record that would be intelligible to his contemporar-

ies and perhaps decipherable by posterity. However, it seems
unlikely that he would have painted these pictures for information. The appearance and habits of the animals that he was
depicting were known just as well to his fellow hunters as
they were to the artist himself; and this knowledge was inti-
mate; for the hunters were dependent on their prey for their
entire livelihood. They fed themselves on its flesh; they
clothed themselves with its skin and fur; and they made tools
from its bones and its sinews. We may therefore guess that the
purpose of these cave paintings was operational. The hunter
perhaps believed that depicting the animal gave him power
over it and thus improved his chances of successful hunting.

The purpose of ritual dancing and singing is undoubtedly
operational. The dancing of David before the Ark, of Ethiopian
Christian priests on Easter morning, and of Japanese priests
and priestesses at the Shinto shrine at Ise is surely intended
to activate the numinous powers and to bring the human participants in the ritual into communion with these powers. In
primitive ritual acts there is not yet any distinction between
clerical officiants and lay spectators. There are no mere spectators; all members of the community are actively engaged in the
performance.

Present-day Western "psychedelic" music and dancing, accompanied by a hypnotizing play of colored lights, has the
same purpose as religious dancing and singing, though the
effect is produced at an ultra-primitive prereligious level of
psychic action. The objective is to enable the participants
temporarily to submerge their individual conscious personali-
ties and to enter into communion with each other through the
"collective unconscious." This modern Western form of operational communicative art has parallels and precedents in Pales-
tine, Asia Minor, and Greece. The common feature is that the
performers work themselves into a state of ecstasy or frenzy,
and that this mood is infectious. Saul was psychically in-
fected by an encounter with a band of ecstatic prophets, and
he was subject to recurrent bouts of this frenzy for the rest
of his life. The Pythia at Delphi fell into a trance for deliver-

ing the god Apollo's oracles, and the bacchant devotees of the
god Dionysus went wild as they roamed over the mountains.
This form of infectious ecstasy has been particularly persist-
ent in Asia Minor. It has manifested itself there in the pre-
Christian votaries of Cybele and Attis, in the Montanist Christian prophetesses of the second century, and in the Moslem
Mevlevi "dancing dervishes," who continued to perform till the
nineteen-twenties, when they were banned in the modernizing
revolution carried out by Mustafa Kemal Atatürk.

Alternatively, art—especially visual art—can be used as a
medium for conveying information. In a preliterate society, this
is the only medium available besides the recitation of oral poetry; and pictures, bas-reliefs, and statues have an important
advantage that oral recitation lacks. They are permanent,
whereas recitation is ephemeral and has constantly to be
repeated if the poetry is to be preserved.

A present-day Western visitor to Ethiopia will find the inner walls of the principal churches covered with pictures.
The main subject is the Bible story, but this merges into
incidents in the lives of the saints, and these merge, in turn,
into current history. A picture of Saint George slaying the
mythical dragon leads on to one of the Emperor Haile Selassie
slaying the Italian dragon. If the church is a famous one, at
Addis Ababa or in one of the major rural monasteries, the visitor will see a stream of country people walking round the
church and looking at the pictures. As far as a foreign onlooker can judge, these Ethiopian country people are a cross
between pilgrims and sightseers, but their sightseeing is not
frivolous; it is partly devout and also partly self-educational.
The pictures in the churches are the Ethiopian peasant's
books, and there will be priests in attendance who will explain to him the subject of any picture that is not familiar
enough for him to be able to identify it for himself.

In watching this contemporary Ethiopian scene, the Western
observer is obtaining a retrospective view of his own medieval
past. It was in just this spirit that his illiterate European
ancestors gazed at the sculptures and the stained-glass win-

dows of the cathedral at Chartres, and this was one of the historic functions of all the churches and temples of most of the religions in the World. (Judaism and, following in its wake, Islam have been exceptional in banning the visual representation of living creatures.) Walk round the Old Metropolitan Church at Athens or the monastic church on Akhtamar Island in Lake Van, or visit as recent a religious building as King Henry VII's chapel at Westminster Abbey. Here at Westminster you will see, juxtaposed, two worlds which were contemporary chronologically but which belong to two different epochs. Here the Italian Renaissance jostles with the Middle Ages; yet, for all its diversity, the wealth of sculpture in this chapel serves a common traditional purpose. At the dawn of the age of printing, it provided a decipherable equivalent of a book for a still mainly illiterate population.

In an Ethiopian church today there are priests in attendance, as has been mentioned, to act as the pilgrims' mentors. The scene of the fifth-century B.C. Athenian dramatist Euripides' play *Ion* is laid in the temple of Apollo at Delphi. The chorus consists of Athenian pilgrims, and they are taking delight in identifying for themselves, unaided, the subjects of the bas-reliefs with which the temple is decorated. Informational communicative art is probably younger than operational communicative art, but it too has played a historic role which in Ethiopia is not yet obsolete.

In what way does "communicative" art differ from "esoteric" art? On first thoughts we might be tempted to suppose that the contrast between these two kinds of art is identical with the contrast between naturalistic art on the one hand and stylized or abstract art on the other hand. Surely, we might say to ourselves, an art that simulates nature must be communicative in the sense of being intelligible to everyone, whereas an art that is stylized or abstract will be intelligible only to people who hold the key to it, and these are likely to be a minority. Actually, the history of art tells us that the truth is exactly the reverse of this. "Naturalism," so far from being natural and therefore self-explanatory, is sophisticated, and is therefore enigmatic to the uninitiated. Where and when a naturalistic form of art has arisen in the past, it has always started as the work of a small sophisticated minority and has been in danger of remaining esoteric unless the exponents of naturalism have succeeded in converting the public at large to viewing the world through the naturalistic artist's sophisticated eyes.

Naturalism is unnatural because every child, and, in primitive societies, every adult too, wants to see reality represented as it really is, and we all know that reality is three-dimensional and that the two-dimensional simulation of it in a picture is a clever artistic sleight of hand. The unsophisticated viewer wants to walk round an object and to see it three-dimensionally by looking at it successively from different angles. He can do this, of course, with a statue in the round, but not with a bas-relief or with a picture. So for the child and for the primitive adult two-dimensional visual art is at best unsatisfying and at worst unintelligible. For him the satisfactory pictorial representation of a cube would be one that displayed all six sides of the cube at once, though it is impossible to see more than three of them at once and, even so, the view of these three is partial and is distorted.

Assyrian winged bulls are standing still as seen from a front view but are walking as seen from a side view, so they have to be given five legs (only five, because one of the legs does double duty; it serves both the front view and the side view; the bull would have had to be given eight legs if he had been standing free, but he needs five only, because one of his flanks was originally pressed against a wall and was therefore invisible). "Verism," which, as the meaning of the word indicates, is "trueness to life" for a sophisticated eye, may be puzzling or actually incomprehensible for a naïve eye. The naïve eye finds "veristic" presentations difficult to interpret because they present things as they look, and not as the primitive knows that they really are.

Naturalism has been introduced a number of times, but it has not always found acceptance. It was introduced in Pharaonic Egypt in the fourteenth century B.C. by the personal choice and fiat of the revolutionary Pharaoh Akhenaton, but it was abandoned in the counterrevolution after Akhenaton's death. The Egyptians then reverted to their traditional style. To modern eyes—even to postnaturalistic modern eyes—this style looks artificial, but for the Egyptian people it was, or had come to be, the intelligible way of representing objects visually. Naturalism has gained widespread popular acceptance at two times and places only: in the Graeco-Roman world for rather less than seven centuries beginning in the early fifth century B.C., and in the modern Western world for about the same length of time, starting in Giotto's generation in the thirteenth century of the Christian Era. The modern bout of naturalism was inspired by the surviving monuments of the Graeco-Roman bout, so, in a sense, the Graeco-Roman case is a unique instance of a successful new departure along this road, and it is significant that, in both these cases, there has been a recoil from naturalism when this has been carried to its farthest possible lengths. The Graeco-Roman world recoiled from it toward the close of the third century of the Christian Era, and the modern Western world in the twentieth century.

In both these cases the abandonment of naturalism was not due to a loss of the technique for producing naturalistic drawings, paintings, mosaics, and sculptures. We know the facts in the case of the twentieth-century rebels against naturalism. All the most eminent of them, at any rate, started as naturalists in the traditional style and demonstrated their proficiency in this style before they revolted against it. It is warrantable to infer that in the third-century revolt it was the same story; for the latest of the third-century works of Graeco-Roman art in the naturalistic style are both extremely competent and studiously "veristic." Manifestly these Graeco-Roman artists, like their twentieth-century counterparts, were masters of the naturalistic technique and could have gone on producing works in that style if they had chosen to.

In both cases the rejection of naturalism was deliberate. The rebel artists were sophisticated in the sense that their change of style was conscious. The change was startling to their contemporaries because it was a sharp break with a long-established and therefore familiar convention. But, though their style was startling and was also shocking to the conventional-minded, it was not esoteric; for they were trying to express an attitude to life, a state of feeling, and a yearning that were common to them and to a majority of their public, and in this the artists were truly representative of their public, though they were in advance of it and were giving it a lead, in virtue of their artistic gift. They were rebelling against naturalism because they felt that it was unsatisfactory for themselves and also sensed that it was unsatisfactory for their public as well.

The reason why naturalism was jettisoned in the third century A.D. was because the contemporary generation of Graeco-Roman society had become interested no longer in portraying the human body as it looks, but in trying to express the ethos of the human soul through a portrayal of the human body as it does *not* look (e.g., by exaggerating the size of the eyes and by giving them an unrealistically intense expression).

This revolution in Graeco-Roman art was sudden and violent because it was a long-delayed response to a change of heart that had been taking place gradually, but with a cumulative effect, in the Graeco-Roman society. Early-fifth-century-B.C. naturalism had been an expression of the Greeks' delight in, and confidence in, the particular form of society that they had succeeded in creating for themselves—a society in which the key institution was the city-state. But within little more than half a century of the triumph of naturalistic art in the Greek world this happiness had begun to be marred, and this confidence to be undermined, by the first of a series of political and social crises that were accompanied and aggravated by atrocities of ever-increasing enormity. There was a series of these self-inflicted disasters because the Greeks failed lamentably to cope with one disaster after another. They did not learn the lesson offered by suffering, or, in so far as they did learn it, they did not take it to heart and therefore did not act on it effectively.

This Greek "time of troubles" was eventually brought to an end by the imposition of the Roman Peace, but this was imposed by such brutal means and at such a fearful cumulative cost that peace and law and order, when they were established at last, were able to give the Graeco-Roman society only a temporary reprieve, not a genuine recovery from its desperate social and spiritual sickness. When the Roman Peace, in its turn, suffered its first big breakdown in the third century A.D., the people of the Roman Empire finally despaired of life in this world, which had seemed so promising to the Greeks in the early fifth century B.C. In reaction to successive shocks, the Greeks and Romans had been transferring their spiritual treasure from the world of social relations to the world of the individual soul's inner life. In psychological terms, they had been becoming introvert instead of extrovert. The whole of this long span of tragic historical experience was expressed in the artistic revolution toward the close of the third century A.D. The expression was sudden, but the change of mood that was now expressed had been maturing over a course of centuries.

The modern Western world, too, has had its self-inflicted disasters and atrocities. In retrospect, the outbreak of the First World War in 1914 may perhaps be seen to have been a turning-point of the same significance as the outbreak of the Great Atheno-Peloponnesian War in 431 B.C. However, in the nineteen-seventies the modern West's "time of troubles" is still relatively young, and the iron has not yet entered deep into our souls. The twentieth-century recoil from naturalism in modern Western art looks less like a reaction to the breakdown of Western politics and morals than like a reaction to the contemporary triumph of Western science and technology.

Modern Western man has made nonsense of the naturalistic style of Western art by crushing nature both in his environment and in himself. One of the innumerable ways in which he has subdued nature has been his discovery of technological means of simulating her. Color photography has achieved a degree of "verism" with which the most skillful artist cannot vie. Accordingly the artist, now foiled in his traditional field of achievement, has set himself new goals, and modern man's scientific and technological prowess has determined, for the artist, what these new goals shall be. The scientific-technological revolution has now gone so far that it has virtually obliterated man's natural environment by imposing an artificial, man-made environment upon nature. Twentieth-century Western artists who have broken away from the modern Western naturalistic tradition are simulating in their works the "other world" that science and technology have conjured up. This other world is a new heaven and a new earth, but, unlike the introvert art that eventually conquered the traditional extrovert Graeco-Roman art, the art that is expressing the modern new world is not in a new dimension. Present-day Westerners are still in the middle of their own story. We cannot read our own future. But if our future were to prove as tragic as the closing chapters of Graeco-Roman history, it is conceivable that Western art, in its turn, might undergo a further revolution that would be of the same kind, and the same magnitude, as the third-century revolution in Graeco-Roman art.

In any case, the West has already followed suit to the Graeco-Roman world in rejecting naturalism, and we can see that in both cases the rebel artists were not cutting themselves off from their public. So far from that, they were giving artistic expression to feelings, thoughts, and desires that they shared with their public. They were not deviating from the course on which their public's feet were set; they were actually anticipating this course.

The recoil from naturalism, then, is not the same thing as esotericism. The true meaning of esotericism is the rejection of a common vehicle of communication between the artist and the majority of the members of his society. Esotericism is the use of an idiom that is private either to some single artist or to members of some small coterie. The criterion of esotericism is not style; it is the artist's attitude toward his relation to his public when he has created a new style. Innovation is the consequence of creativity, and good innovations are potential boons for mankind. But the artist who has made a revolutionary innovation is confronted with a choice that is a challenge and a test. Shall the creative artist be a missionary, or shall he be a recluse? Shall he make it his concern to communicate his new insight to his public, or shall he keep his discovery to himself or, at most, extend his communication of it to a narrow circle of his cronies?

The missionary seeks to be *not* esoteric, and, if he is in earnest, he may succeed in re-entering into communion with the rest of society, even though the style that he is propagating may be highly conventional or highly abstract. Conversely, the deliberate recluse will be esoteric, even if the style that he is keeping to himself is one that his fellow members of society could appreciate and might be ready to adopt with alacrity if only the artist were willing to share his treasure with them. On this test, an ultra-naturalistic artist can be an ultra-esoteric one at the same time.

The Graeco-Roman artists who revolted against naturalism in the conventional meaning of the word had recognized that nature, besides including the tangible, visible, and apparently external physical world, includes as well an inner psychic world—the psyche's subconscious abyss. There is, of course, more than one way of trying to express psychic nature. The revolutionaries who substituted the Byzantine style of art for the Graeco-Roman style created symbols for psychic realities by a nonnaturalistic presentation of the human body's physical features. In our time, James Joyce has tried another method. He has sought to convey the essence of psychic nature not symbolically but naturalistically. He has set himself to simulate the flow of subconscious psychic activity. (The ultra-veristic technological counterpart of Joyce's artistic style is automatic writing.)

Actually, Joyce, like the Byzantine icon-painters, has to resort to symbolism. Perhaps psychic reality can be represented only in some symbolic form or other. The Byzantines symbolized psychic reality by distorting the shape of the human form; Joyce symbolized it by distorting the shapes of words. We

need not question the legitimacy of either of these devices for
symbolizing by distortion. The Byzantine artists, however,
were missionaries who succeeded in making the symbols that
they had created into the common property of the society in
and for which they worked. Joyce, and other writers of the
same modern Western school, have remained recluses so far.
They have portrayed a private world of their own, without
attempting to make it communicable by translating it into
a common idiom.

The activity that goes on in the subconscious abyss of the
psyche is, of course, a private world in the raw form in which
it wells up into the consciousness of an individual human being. It is not only private; it is often unintelligible even to
the person who experiences it, unless and until it is interpreted for him—and therefore potentially for the public at
large—by a professional psychologist. Part of the psychologist's task is to translate the revealed contents of the subconscious into an idiom that is common to the psychologist,
his patient, and the public. Perhaps this task can be accom-
plished only approximately and imperfectly. The irrational
world of the subconscious psyche and the rational world of
man the social animal may be to some extent incommensurable.
At the same time, there are contents in the subconscious that
are common to all human beings, and are therefore perhaps
translatable into a common rational idiom, if C. G. Jung is right
in holding that, bedded deep in the subconscious, there are
"primordial images" which are intrinsic to human nature itself.

Our criticism of modern writers of the school represented by
Joyce is that they have not tried, so far, to do in the realm
of art what the psychologists are trying to do in the realm of
science. These artists are not trying to work up the raw materials of their art into a communicable form, or, at most, they
are content to share them with a small and unrepresentative
coterie. This is true esotericism, and some, at least, of its
manifestations are almost wantonly perverse. Examples of deliberate obscurity are the abstruse literary allusions in the

poetry of Robert Browning (to a relatively moderate extent) and of modern poets of a later generation such as Ezra Pound and T. S. Eliot. A similar example is Joyce's title *Ulysses* and his covert reproduction of the plot of the *Odyssey.*

It should be noted in this connection that there is nothing esoteric in allusions to the Qur'an in Islamic literature or to the Bible and the Greek and Latin classical authors in medieval and early modern Western Christian literature. Milton's poetry, for instance, is not esoteric, since Milton was addressing a public to which the Bible and the classics were as familiar as they were to him. Milton's poetry has become esoteric posthumously, because the Bible and the classics have now ceased to be familiar to the educated public in the Western world, but—unlike Eliot and Pound—Milton was not esoteric deliberately, and, if he could have foreknown that he would eventually become esoteric against his own intentions, he would not have been gratified; he would have been distressed.

Alexandrian Greek literature, on the other hand, was deliberately esoteric in the manner of some recent Western poets. In Roman literature, which was influenced by Alexandrianism, the word "learnèd" (*doctus*) was a laudatory epithet for poets. In English it is a standing epithet for lawyers, and, though it is laudatory when used by lawyers among themselves, such "learnedness" is not a virtue in the eyes of the "lay" public. It is one of the scandals of law—particularly of uncodified law—that, though it affects the lives of ordinary people, it is beyond the layman's understanding and has to be interpreted for him by professionals. It cannot be good that art should become a preserve for learnèd professionals, such as law is.

An extreme form of learnèd esotericism is archaism. Examples from the history of the Graeco-Roman world are the neo-Atticism of the latest age of ancient Greek literature, the pseudo-archaic Greek statues with which the Emperor Hadrian furnished his villa in the second century of the Christian Era, and the neo-archaic Latin in which the Emperor Marcus Aurelius's tutor Fronto wrote at a later date in the same cen-

tury. Examples from the history of architecture and visual art
in the modern West are the nineteenth-century Pre-Raphaelite
English school of painting; the touches of West African art
in some modern Western sculpture; and the Mayan style of
Frank Lloyd Wright's Imperial Hotel in Tokyo (pulled down in
1967 against the protests of Japanese connoisseurs who treasured it as a "period piece").

The form taken by esotericism in religion is "gnosis";
i.e., abstruse knowledge of the truths that are the means of
salvation—a knowledge which, just because of its supposedly
inestimable value, is communicated to the initiated only, as a
secret that is to be jealousy guarded. In the Greek world the
Eleusinian Mysteries were a case of "gnosis" that anticipated the "gnostic" movement of the second century of the
Christian Era.

Esotericism has its nemesis, but fortunately the nemesis can
be averted by an antidote.

The nemesis is that when artists work only for themselves
individually or for a coterie, and disdain the public, the public
retorts by ignoring the esoteric artists, and the vacuum thus
created is then filled by charlatans. This is bad for the public
and bad for the artists too. Modern Western society is exposed
to this danger because its sensational success in science and
technology has been bought at the price of extreme professional
specialization, and this is an obstacle to communication. Its
effect is to break society up into cliques that are incomprehensible to each other.

The remedy for this evil is that the person who is compelled
by the modern Western way of life to become a specialist in the
work by which he earns his living should make a point of edu-
cating himself to be a generalist when he is off duty. This is
going to be practicable, because automation is going to reduce working hours drastically. More and more people are
going to be paid a wage on which they will be well off for a
regimen in which there will be less work than leisure. If we
are wise, we shall find in this unprecedented leisure an opportunity for making ourselves into intelligent generalists—

that is to say, into potentially good citizens of the world. The public that is needed in the modern world is a public that will take an intelligent interest in all human affairs in spite of the fact that every member of this public will be a "layman" in every department except his own narrow professional patch of specialization.

The importance of catering for this intelligent "lay" public, and of fostering its advance in degree of culture and its increase in numbers, has never been lost sight of by French savants and artists. Artistic and intellectual standards in France are the highest in the world, yet French "highbrows" have never felt it to be beneath their dignity to produce *œuvres de vulgarisation.* The word *vulgarisation,* used in this sense, is only ironically self-deprecatory. Some of the most eminent French savants have put their best work into this important intellectual and social task of maintaining their lines of communication with their public.

Here France has set an example which the rest of the world ought to take to heart. When the "intellectuals" become alienated from the intelligent "lay" public, this is a symptom of a serious cultural malady. No society can afford to let this malady increase unchecked. If it is allowed to go to extremes, the consequence for society is rebarbarization.

Silence to Light

(Light to Silence)

The desire to express (the meeting of)

The Threshold

The Inspirations
The Sanctuary of Art
The Treasury of The Shadows

Architecture:
Silence and Light

LOUIS I. KAHN

As one of America's most influential architects, Mr. Kahn has designed buildings both here and abroad and has taught at both Yale University and the University of Pennsylvania.

Let us go back in time to the building of the pyramids. Hear the din of industry in a cloud of dust marking their place. Now we see the pyramids in full presence. There prevails the feeling of Silence, in which is felt man's desire to express. This existed before the first stone was laid.

I note that when a building is being made, free of servitude, its spirit to be is high—no blade of grass can grow in its wake. When the building stands complete and in use, it seems to want to tell you about the adventure of its making. But all the parts locked in servitude make this a story of little interest. When its use is spent and it becomes a ruin, the wonder of its beginning appears again. It feels good to have itself entwined in foliage, once more high in spirit and free of servitude.

I sense Light as the giver of all presences, and material as spent Light. What is made by Light casts a shadow, and the shadow belongs to Light. I sense a Threshold: Light to Silence, Silence to Light—an ambiance of inspiration, in which the desire to be, to express crosses with the possible. The rock, the stream, the wind inspires. We see what is beautiful in the mate-

The one desires To be to express The one

Eternity is of two Brothers

to be to make The one light

Non Luminous The one light Luminous

Spending to the emmergance of Material

The prevailing luminous

Groups to remite a vivid domes

Of flaming prevalance

Architecture is the making
of a room; an assembly
of rooms. The light is the
light of that room.
Thoughts exchanged by
one and another are not
the same in one room as
in another.
A street is a room; a community room by agreement
Its character from intersection to intersection changes
and may be regarded as a number of rooms

rial first in wonder, then in knowing, which in turn is transformed into the expression of beauty that lies in the desire to express. Light to Silence, Silence to Light crosses in the sanctuary of art. Its treasury knows no favorite, knows no style. Truth and rule out of commonness, law out of order are the offerings within.

Architecture has no presence but exists as the realization of a spirit. A work of architecture is made as an offering reflecting the nature of that spirit. One can also say that the realms of painting, sculpture, and literature exist in spirit, their natures revealed by works that are unfamiliar. In using the word "unfamiliar," I recognize the singularity of every individual in attitude and talent. But the phenomena of individual realizations of a spirit are only new images of that same spirit. So it is in nature that the diversity of forms evolves from universal order.

Form is the recognition of an integrity of inseparable elements. This is true in both nature and art. In nature validity is nonconscious. Every grain of sand on the beach has a natural color and shape, is of natural weight and in its natural position. It is part of the constant play of equilibria, governed solely by the laws of nature. What man makes must answer to the laws of nature, and is governed in his concepts by rules and choice. The one is measurable. The one is completely unmeasurable. What nature makes, it makes without man, and what man makes, nature cannot make without him.

Nature does not make a house. It cannot make a room. How marvelous that when I am in a room with another the mountains, trees, wind, and rain leave us for the mind, and the room becomes a world in itself. With only one other person one feels generative. The meeting becomes an event. The actor throws aside the lines of his performance. The residue from all his thoughts and experiences meets the other on equal terms. Even now, though I feel I am saying things differently from the way I have said them before, I have thought about them and the idea is therefore not essentially generative. The room, then, is a marvelous thing.

Architecture deals primarily with the making of spaces to serve the institutions of man. In the aura of Silence and Light, the desire to be, to make, to express, recognizes the laws that confirm the possible. Strong, then, is the desire to know, heralding the beginning of the institutions of learning dedicated to discover how we were made. In man is the record of man. Man through his consciousness feels this record, which sparks his desire to learn what nature has given him and what choices he has made to protect himself and his desires in the odyssey of his emergence.

I believe that consciousness is in all life. It is in the rose, in the microbe, in the leaf. Their consciousness is not understandable to us. How much more would we comprehend if we were to uncover their secrets, for then a wider sense of commonness would enter expressions in art, giving the artist greater insight in presenting his offerings answering to the prevailance of order, the prevailance of commonness.

Dissension is out in the open. I do not feel that its roots come from need alone. Dissension stems from desire— desire for what is not yet made, not yet expressed. Need comes from the known. Supplying only what is lacking brings no lasting joy. Did the world need the Fifth Symphony before Beethoven wrote it? Did Beethoven need it? He desired it, and now the world needs it. Desire brings about the new need.

I look at the glancing light on the side of the mountain, which is such a meaningful light, bringing every tiny natural detail to the eye, and teaching us about material and choice in making a building. But do I get less delight out of seeing a brick wall with all its attempts at regularity, its delightful imperfections revealed in natural light? A wall is built in the hope that a light once observed may strike it again in a rare moment in time. How can anyone imagine a building of spaces not seen in natural light? Schools are being built with little or no natural light, supposedly to save on maintenance costs and to assure the teachers of their pupils' undivided attention. The most wonderful aspects of the indoors are the moods

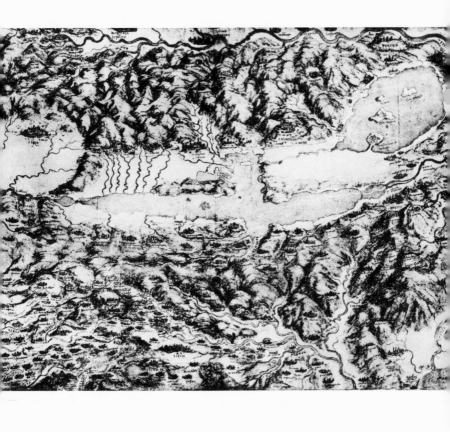

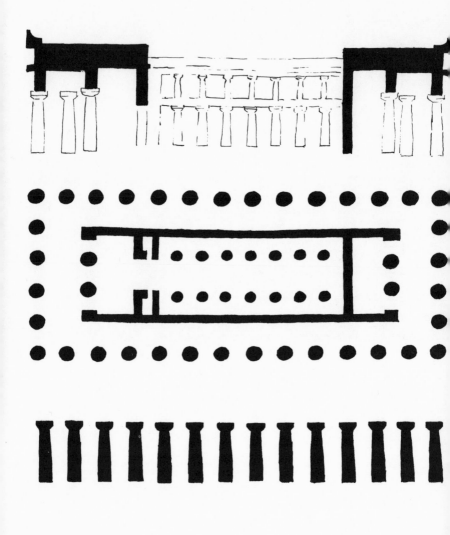

that light gives to space. The electric bulb fights the sun. Think of it.

I am reminded of Tolstoi, who deviated from faithlessness to faith without question. In his latter state he deplored the miracles, saying that Christ has radiance without them. They were holding a candle to the sun to see the sun better.

Structure is the maker of light. A column and a column bring light between them. It is darkness-light, darkness-light, darkness-light, darkness-light. In the column we realize a simple and beautiful rhythmic beauty evolved from the primitive wall and its openings. At first, walls were thick. They protected man. He felt the desire for freedom and the promise of the world outside. He made at first a rude opening. Then he explained to the unhappy wall that, in accepting an opening, the wall must now follow a higher order with arches and piers as new and worthy elements. These are the realizations in architecture of Light and Structure. The choice of a square room is also the choice of its light as distinguished from other shapes and their light. Even a room which must be dark needs at least a crack of light to know how dark it is. But architects in planning rooms today have forgotten their faith in natural light. Depending on the touch of a finger to a switch, they are satisfied with static light and forget the endlessly changing qualities of natural light, in which a room is a different room every second of the day.

I spoke of form as the realization of a nature. A shape is an expression of form. Form follows desire as a realization of a dream or a belief. Form tells of inseparable elements. Design is the struggle to develop these elements into shapes compatible with each other, reaching for a wholeness, for a name. Form in the mind of one is not the same as it is in the mind of another. The realization of a nature, form, and shape are not part of the process of design-manipulation. In design there are wonderful realizations: the order of structure, the order of construction, the order of time, the order of spaces come into play.

As I see a sheet of music, I realize that the musician sees it to hear. To an architect, the plan is a sheet on which appears the order of the structure of spaces in their light.

The institutions of learning give the architect a program of requirements. These requirements are derived from previous plans which were designed to answer momentary needs. These needs are very far from the original spirit School. The architect must consider the program merely as a guide. The spirit School, in the sense of its conceived commonness, should be considered as though it is being realized for the first time.

Recently my class decided to speculate on the question: what is a university? We had no program. We thought of the nature of a university. Our minds were empty of knowing and full of adventure. One student gave emphasis to the central library as the place of the dedication of the mind. It was suggested also that the libraries of the different professions should be related to the main library by a conscious "Architecture of Connection," since the university's most direct service to the community is the sanctioning of the professions. But we were distressed because we realized that the university is gradually falling into the sphere of the marketplace, competing with other schools for research money and inventing special degrees to attract students. Architecture, for instance, is being separated from urban design and city-planning and thus shutting off students with broad natural talents in architecture, who refuse to accept such professional distinctions.

In the marketplace the professions tend to become businesses which suppress individual talent, whose leadership has always been followed. The architect can realize the spirit of his art and the emerging orders only when the problems before him are considered as part of a whole. Relegated to niches of specialization, he will become one of a team, designing parts and giving the world nothing but solutions of immediate needs. He will never be free or experienced enough to guide prevailing desires to inspirations. Although I feel that unique talent cannot be overthrown, it is hurt by being retarded. Talent has to be recognized early to do good work.

Each stroke of the pen is where the light is not

In considering the architecture of connection—library to library—my students developed their thoughts about the significant places to be found in the university. The garden became inseparable from the room, the court, the entrance place of invitation, the green or the great court as the place of the happening.

Dissensions made us think of a place or a structure not yet named for the teacher, the student, and the directors. Like the stoa, it would not be partitioned, and its position on the campus would be on a great lawn with not a path crossing it. The division would be agreed upon later and the lawn modified by the use it evoked.

It was thought that a university has much to gain from the city, which in turn may consider the university as one of its most important institutions. But professional practice is in the marketplace, and the university in sanctioning the professions should be free of it. This brought to our minds the role of the city-planner. We realized that there must be a place free of the university and free of the marketplace where both could meet. The visions of planners meet the political economy of the city. This separate place should be recognized as a new institution of man, equal to the institutions of government, of learning, and of health.

The city is measured by its institutions, and its growth is felt in the works of its leaders who are sensitive to the desires of the people and who want to serve their desire for expression. The studies leading to the emergence of new institutions become the points of departure for planning. Movement plans and redevelopment schemes are merely corrective projects. The known institutions need new vitality, conscious recognition. As an example of current deterioration, think of City Hall, which evolved from the early meeting place on the village green. It is probably the most dishonored building in the city —a place associated with taxes, fees, courts, and jails, where nobody meets. Since the day of the meeting house, the interests of people have become greatly extended and diversified, but there is no place for us to air these interests. A place of auditoria, meeting rooms, and seminars would revive the spirit of representation and give every man a place which he feels is his own city house.

Our inspirations assist us when we clear our senses of known solutions and methods. The realization of a yet unthought-of nature and the elements of its form can stimulate an entirely new point of view about everything. Today we talk about technology as though our minds will be surrendered to the machine. Surely the machine is merely a brain which we get, pot luck, from nature. But a mind capable of realization can inspire a new technology and humiliate the current one.

Teaching is a work. The beginning is dear to the teacher, for he senses what man is from what he accepts and is willing to support. The code of the teacher is often remote from another man's. Because of his desire to tell about his mind, he seeks words that are as close to his code as possible without losing generativeness. I have used "commonness" instead of "spirit" for that very reason. Spirit is immediately assumed as understood. Commonness makes one think.

Art is the making of a life. When we hear the strains of a familiar musical masterpiece, it is as though a familiar person entered the room. But as you must see him again in order to believe his presence, so must the music be played again so you can remember all that touched you before.

In Mexico I met the architect Barragan. I was impressed by his work because of its closeness to nature. His garden is framed by a high private wall, the land and foliage remaining untouched as he found it. In it is a fountain made by a water source lightly playing over a jagged splinter and, drop for drop, falling in a great bowl of rhinoceros-gray-black stone filled to the brim. Each drop was like a slash of silver making rings of silver reaching for the edge and falling to the ground. The water in the black container was a choice from the path of water as a mountain stream in light, over rocks, and then in deep seclusion where its silver was revealed. He learned about water and selected what he loved most.

His house is not merely a house but house itself. Any

one could feel at home. Its material is traditional, its character eternal. We talked about traditions as though they were mounds of golden dust of man's nature, from which circumstances were distilled out. As man takes his path through experience, he learns about man. Learning falls as golden dust, which if touched gives the power of anticipation. The artist has this power and knows the world even before it began. He expresses himself in terms of psychological validities.

A student once asked, "What is the intuitive sense?" Robert le Ricolais, mathematician, engineer, and scientist, answered, "What made man venture to make the first thing? Surely it was not his knowledge but his sense of validity. But intuition must be fed. I might say that everything must begin with poetry."

The illustrations accompanying this essay were made especially for this book by the author, with the exception of those on pages 27, 29, and 32, which are identified as follows: Leonardo da Vinci's map of part of Central Italy; a holograph page of Beethoven's Sonata No. 32 in C-Minor, Opus III; and one of George Cruikshank's engravings illustrating The Waverly Novels.

Art and the Structuralist Perspective

ANNETTE MICHELSON

Miss Michelson has studied art history at Columbia and philosophy at the Sorbonne. She now teaches the Aesthetics of Cinema at the Graduate School of the Arts of New York University, and her articles on art and film have been widely published in this country and Europe.

Years ago, when I was a student, I happened to see an entry in a bookseller's catalogue for an edition of Kant's *Critique of Pure Reason* described as "beautiful" and "illustrated." That entry caught my fancy, produced a kind of mental cramp, and intrigued me so that I eventually made the trip down to Fourth Avenue to have a look at the book. But not, of course, before I'd spent some time trying to relax that cramp, speculating upon the order and imagining the style of those illustrations.

This kind of tension recurred quite recently when, reading through the theoretical writings of Eisenstein, I came across notes on a project for a filmed version of Marx's *Das Kapital*. History—the history of Marxism, in fact—has deprived us all of this version. The man does not live who can say, "No, I haven't read the book, but I've seen the movie." What, however, might that movie be? How is one to imagine its form, describe its possible contours? The nineteenth-century novel does offer some partial dramatizations—of the celebrated chapter on the working day, among others. And Brecht, I think, provides the closest aesthetic exemplification of Marxist analytic method; the formal strategy of the distancing or alienation effect suggests itself as a powerful instance. Can one, however, proceed to figure the idea of plus value? Or a sentence such as the following: "It is value . . . that converts every product of labor into a social hieroglyph?"

As for the illustrated edition of the *Critiques,* I remember that my speculations—more like musing, really—tended to center about notions and images of geometric forms, those which are described in the *Philebus* as the truest, and consequently the most beautiful, of figures. "What I mean," says Socrates, "what the argument points to, is something straight or round, and the surfaces and solids which a lathe or carpenter's rule and square produces from the straight and round. I wonder if you understand. Things of that sort, I maintain, are beautiful, not, like most things, in a relative sense; they are always beautiful in their very nature, and they offer pleasures peculiar to themselves, and quite unlike others. They have that purity which makes for truth. They are philosophical."[1]

Plato, of course, never conceived the notion of those "philosophical things" or geometrical forms as providing the substance and vocabulary of art itself. An art of "pure plastics," that ultimate variant of aesthetic idealism, was unknown to him. It was, however, familiar to me, and I enjoyed, then, fancying an illustrated edition of the *Critiques* as a series of Icons of the Rational. Although that cramp was not relaxed entirely by thoughts of late Mondrian and Kandinsky, I remember that my imaginings were tinted by them. I actually fancied these two distinguished disciples of Madame Blavatsky as Iconographers of the Rational! I was wrong, of course, for when I got down to Fourth Avenue and opened the volume, I saw that the illustration consisted of a frontispiece, a portrait of Kant. I should have anticipated this but did not, and it now occurs to me that I probably did not want to, because the imagining had involved a game, a very primitive exercise in sign theory or semiology.

[1] *Philebus,* translated by R. Hackworth, in *The Collected Dialogues of Plato Including the Letters,* edited by Edith Hamilton and Huntingdon Cairns, Bollingen Series LXXI (New York: Pantheon Books, 1963), p. 1132.

Piet Mondrian: *Composition*, 1929.
The Solomon R. Guggenheim Museum, New York

Vasily Kandinsky: *Pronounced Rose No. 573*, 1932.
The Solomon R. Guggenheim Museum, New York

Engraved portrait
of Immanuel Kant

The notion of an illustrated edition of the *Critiques* seems, in any case, to have slumbered on in me until much later when, opening a volume of the writings of Claude Lévi-Strauss, I came upon some plates which seemed to offer closer approximations of an illustrated edition of Kant that the engraving of the Philosopher himself. Here they are: two diagrams comparing kinship systems of primitive tribes.

And how can these be said to constitute effective Icons of the Rational? They represent an attempt, initiated by Kant and implemented by the analytic methods of structuralist anthropology, to extend our knowledge of reality, to acquaint us with the manner in which the human mind organizes its experience of the world. Inviting us to explore the dynamics of the mind, they propose an intelligibility of our universe. These diagrams illustrate an undertaking as ambitious and impressive as any that one could conceive. The manner in which that enterprise is articulated and set in motion is something to which we will return. Consider, for the moment, a definition of its aims, as they have informed a life-work covering a vast range

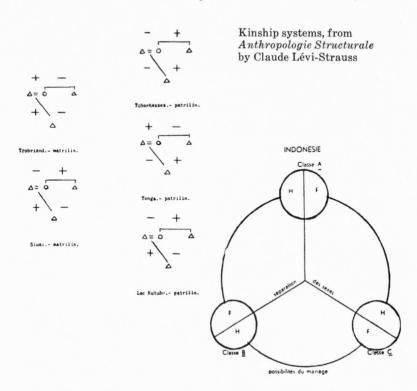

Kinship systems, from
Anthropologie Structurale
by Claude Lévi-Strauss

Tcherkesses.- patrilin.

Trobriand.- matrilin.

Siuai.- matrilin.

Tonga.- patrilin.

Lac Kutubu.- patrilin.

INDONESIE

Classe A

séparation des sexes

Classe B

Classe C

possibilités du mariage

of empirical observation and grounded in linguistic theory,
issuing, through the study of kinship systems in the tribes we
call primitive, through comparative studies of myth, of cook-
ery and table manners, in an epistemology.

The destination remains unchanged; it is still the inven-
tory, based on ethnographic experience, of our mental contours, the reduction of seemingly arbitrary data to an order,
the location of that level upon which necessity, immanent in
the illusions of freedom, is revealed. Beneath the apparent
and superficial randomness, incoherence and diversity characteristic of marriage regulations, we have disclosed, through
our study of Basic Kinship Structures, a few simple principles. Through their application a very complex set of cus-

toms and usages—at first view, seemingly absurd and generally judged as such—was assembled into a meaningful system.[2]

The province of anthropological research is neither that of individual psychology nor that of the social sciences as developed within the context of the Western philosophical tradition. Unlike the philosopher, though sharing his concerns, the anthropologist rejects the hypothesis of universal suppositions, proceeding instead through empirical observation of the innumerable "concrete systems of representations" that animate and structure the social processes of communities.

And since, for the anthropologist—and he is always a man of a given social origin, a particular culture, region and historical period—these systems represent the entire range of possibilities within a given type, he expressly chooses those which seem to differ most sharply, in the hope that the methodological principle used to translate these systems into the terms of his own system—and conversely—will disclose a network of fundamental common constraints. This involves a supreme form of gymnastics in which the exercise of reflection, pushed to its utmost objective limits (since these have first been surveyed, measured and inventoried through research in the field), brings out each muscle and joint of the skeleton, thereby exposing the lineaments of a general anatomic structure. The important thing is that the human mind reveal a structure that is progressively intelligible. We have stressed our effort to transcend the opposition between the physical and mental by placing our investigations on the terrain of the linguistic sign. Indeed, when used in even very small numbers, these signs lend themselves to rigorously arranged combinations capable of translating the entire diversity of felt experience, even to its subtlest nuances.[3]

It is, then, the business of structuralist analysis to reveal the extraordinary propensity of the human mind to organize,

[2] Claude Lévi-Strauss, *Mythologiques I: Le Cru et le Cuit* (Paris: Librairie Plon, 1964), p. 18.
[3] Ibid., p. 19.

through symbolic sign systems, its experience of the world.

Thus structuralism through Lévi-Strauss inherits the aims of rationalism, its methods and metaphors, its stance of objectivity, and the strategies of observational, empirical research. Taking his cue from his master, Rousseau, Lévi-Strauss believes that "when we wish to study men, we must stay close to home, but in order to study man, we must look away, abroad, further into the distance. We must, if we wish to discover the basic, common properties of things, begin by observing the differences between them. The anthropologist departs from the context of his own culture to rediscover it in rebound through observation of foreign cultures. He departs from the notion of a culture evolving in history to study that of a culture bent upon preserving its identity from transformation through time as the highly ritualized, preliterate cultures are.

In his search for the order within and beneath the apparent irrationality of social organization, Lévi-Strauss follows the nineteenth century's movement from belief in transcendent causes to belief in immanent ones. His acknowledged masters are Freud and Marx, who were concerned, like himself, with the logic of the immanent.

Unlike Freud and Marx, however, he is concerned with the dynamics of neither individual psychology nor class structure, but with human thought in its most general aspects; he must locate the threshold of the human, that level at which man, passing from nature into culture, becomes man. And he discovers it not in the manufacture of artifacts but in the constitution, through communication, of the social group, in the structuring of experience through exchange, governed by rules and articulated through signs.

The rule involves the particular or the relative, as opposed to law, which implies the universal. The domain of the rule is culture; that of Universal Law is nature. Looking for the primary level upon which nature and culture fuse, Lévi-Strauss finds it in that rule which is universal throughout all cultures —the prohibition of incest—instituting always, in its immense formal variety, the pre-eminence of the social over the

natural, of the collective over the individual, of organization
and order over the rule of the arbitrary.

Lévi-Strauss observes that rules governing marriage and
kinship systems guarantee exogamy; they institute exchange
and constitute, in themselves, the emergence of culture as a
system of exchanges. It is, as we might have expected, on the
terrain of sexuality that the threshold between the two orders
is necessarily located.

The rule acts, then, not to prohibit, but—and this is most
important—to *guarantee* exchange. In kinship systems, structure alone remains constant. Within them, individual elements
may shift or change respective positions, provided that relationships between them are respected. The taboo on incest,
then, is not biologically functional, as previous anthropological, psychological, and historical theories had assured us.
It simply insures the inevitability of exchange *as such*.

The prohibitions governing language are as universal as
language itself, and we know considerably more about their
origins than about those of kinship systems. Structuralists
suggest that by following the comparison as far as possible
we may hope to penetrate the meaning of these institutions.

Exogamy and language have parallel and essentially positive functions: the establishment of bonds between men that
permit biological organization to be transcended by social organization. Both exogamy and language insure communication with others and integration of the group. The structuralist
is thus led to see sexual relations and language as modes of
communication.

If I dwell upon the fusion of nature and culture in social institutions interpreted in symbolic signs or structures as guarantees of communication, it is because I wish to convey the
importance of the linguistic mode for structuralist analysis, in
order to examine the nature and limits of its consequences for
art and aesthetics. It is the radical quality of his application of
this linguistic model that distinguishes Lévi-Strauss's effort to
illuminate the mechanisms of thought in terms of "primitive,"

preliterate societies which, unlike ours, apply their energy to maintaining the maximum stability of their symbolic systems and institutions. Rejecting the process of perpetual transformation within history, these societies conserve those systems and institutions through ritual, myth, art, language, and custom.

In adopting language as a model of symbolic systems, Lévi-Strauss is indebted to the methods and achievement of structural linguistics inaugurated by the work of Ferdinand de Saussure and extended by the work of the generation of revolutionary critics, aestheticians, and linguists of Russia and Prague. For methodological clues he has looked most particularly to the work of Roman Jakobson, one of the principal animaters of this discipline as it has moved from East to West and back again within our century.

Saussure's conception of linguistics as part of a new, more general science of semiology had been inspired by Emile Durkheim's emphasis on the necessity for the study of signs considered within social context. Saussure saw the linguistic system or code as pre-existent to the individual act of speech or message, therefore commanding logical priority. Communication was understood as operating on the basis of this double articulation of code and message.

For Saussure, the arbitrariness of the individual sign (its unmotivated character) was fundamental. And the importance, the function, of the sign lies primarily in its differences from others in the same system. C. S. Peirce, his American contemporary, extended and articulated the notion of sign, defining several different kinds. Basically, schematically, there are three: icon, index, and symbol. Anything can be the icon of any object in so far as it is like that object and used as a sign or representation of it. An icon is a sign which possesses the characteristic that renders the object significant, even though the object may have no existence. Thus the images we call "likenesses," such as Kant's portrait, are icons, and since the actual existence of the object or referent does not determine iconicity, one might say that an image representing "real toads in imaginary

gardens" would be an icon as well. A diagram is also an icon, in
that it represents the relations of parts in a model by analogous
relations between its own parts. Degrees of iconicity—higher
and lower—exist.

An index is a sign representing a characteristic of its object
in a physical or observable manner, a sign which would lose the
characteristic that makes it a sign if its object were removed,
but which would not lose the characteristic if there were no
one to interpret it. A piece of wood with a bullet hole in it is the
index of a shot; without the shot there would have been no
hole, but the hole is there, whether or not its cause is per-
ceived. A weathercock is an index of the direction of the wind,
in that there is a physical connection between them. Other examples would be footprints in sand, a rap on the door, or any
signal telling us to pay attention. And Jakobson suggests that
medical symptoms are indices, and symptomatology may be considered a study of indexical signs.

Photographic image and cinema, of course, present a particular problem, as they would seem to involve iconic resemblance
to objects they represent. But this resemblance is due to their
being produced under such circumstances that they were physically forced to correspond point by point to nature. Seen in
that aspect, then, they belong to the second class of signs,
those involving physical connection. Overlapping and difference
in degree are, of course, inherent in the nature of signs.

The symbol is the conventional sign—a word, a sentence, a
book—and it has, in Peirce's term, "the force of law"; it is "a
regularity of the indefinite future," linked neither in terms
of likeness to its object, like the icon, nor physically with its
object, like the index. The symbol is connected with its object
by virtue of the idea of the symbolizing mind, without which
no such connection would exist. It is closest to Saussure's notion of the sign as arbitrary, but presents again the problem
of overlapping and definition. The word is the supreme symbolic sign.

Turning, then, from historical immediacy, the structural anthropologist addresses himself, with a lucidity born of a certain

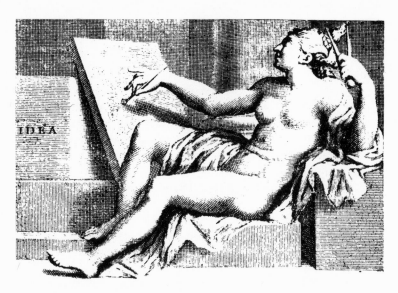

A. Clouwet: *Idea*, 1672, from G. P. Bellori, *Le Vite de' Pittori* ...

guilt, to the study of those societies that his own Western culture had begun to despoil by the sixteenth century. His openness to foreign cultures hinges on his acceptance of himself as rooted in the culture of rationality, of historical progress; he seeks to discover, through analysis of the ritualistic stability of preliterate cultures, something of himself, to scan its mythology for the roots of rationality. Like Rousseau, Lévi-Strauss bears within him a nostalgia born of both that estrangement and that sense of affinity which Panofsky has described as the very essence of the Renaissance sensibility. Like a man of the Renaissance, Lévi-Strauss directs his intellectual heritage, the rationalism of Kant, Rousseau, Marx, Freud, and Cuvier, toward the conquest of knowledge, the dissipation of mystery through the observation of mysteries.

Linguistic method implements the study of social institutions as systems or structures, their nature depending not upon the nature of the individual signs which compose them but on the relationships that organize those signs into meaningful systems.

We may say, then, that structuralists, placing themselves under the auspices of linguistic method and of the sign, adopt a point of view particularly familiar to us, a view of the human mind as possessed by the demon of order. Jakobson and Lévi-Strauss, in fact, describe their subject and method in a way analogous to the means of both artistic creation and art criticism. If it is, indeed, the relating or ordering of differences into a structure which confers interest or value upon signs, we understand the full force of Roman Jakobson's affirmation when, quoting Braque, he says he believes not in things, but in the relationship between things.

Considered within this perspective, classes of objects or institutions within a given culture demand to be treated in terms of their formal coexistence. If, in structuralist analysis —either linguistic or anthropological—the analysis of structures of widely different cultures establishes the existence of common constraints, that is because structuralist analysis places an emphasis on what we term the synchronic aspect of systems—their manner of arrangement, the relationship of parts within the structure—as against the diachronic, the succession of events or elements in time.

Nietzsche had called attention to that hypertrophy of historical consciousness which characterized the nineteenth century. If linguistics and semiology are tending, in our century, to replace history as a dominant discipline, then we must expect a certain uneasiness in reaction to that shift of perspective. And we get it, of course. When structuralism claims the primacy of the synchronic over the diachronic, it points out that history is an abstraction, the positing of a dynamics that cannot in fact be directly deduced from a succession of forms, systems, or structures.

That claim challenges the culture, the sensibility rooted in the historical consciousness of the past century. It challenges the powerfully operative suppositions bequeathed by the last towering philosophical system, that of Hegel. And in France the

Marxist-Hegelian left has responded with a cry of alarm; Sartre reproaches structuralism, in a striking metaphor, for attempting to "replace the moving picture with the magic-lantern slide." I recently observed at a symposium of art historians and historically oriented critics and scholars the extraordinary vividness with which this opposition was rehearsed, and the strong, though unconscious, sense of synchronic perspective as a threat to the aims, methods, and traditions of historical scholarship. That clash now reveals itself in most fields of discourse. If it is to be resolved, it can be so only, I should think, through an acceptance of a complementarity of approach, rather like that involved in the simultaneous admission of both the wave and the corpuscular theories of light in modern physics.

If I have chosen to limit this discussion of the structuralist perspective to a discussion of the work and thought of Lévi-Strauss, and of their implications, it is because he has sought to radicalize the structuralist perspective and activity, extending its province in the service of a supremely ambitious enterprise, and he has done so with a power, elegance, and intellectual tact incomparable in our time.

To confront structuralist perspective in his terms, however, is to confront its deeply problematic and troubling response to the claims, the nature, the facts of modern and modernist art. Here, then, is an initial statement on the art of our age:

. . . one could describe non-figurative painting in terms of two characteristics. The first, which it shares with easel painting, consists in a total rejection of the contingency of destination: the picture is not made for a particular use. [This in contradistinction to the art of primitive societies.] The other, which is proper to non-figurative painting, consists in the methodical exploitation of the contingency of execution, which is claimed as the pretext of the external occasion of the picture. Non-figurative painting adopts manners or styles as its subjects; it claims to present a concrete representation of the formal conditions of all painting. The result is a paradox in that non-figurative painting does not,

as it believes, create works as real as—or more so than—the
objects of the physical world, but realist imitations of non-
existent models. It is an academic school of painting in which
each artist strains after the representation of the manner in
which he would execute his pictures if he happened to be
painting any.[4]

That statement is followed by another, elsewhere, that same
year.

Impressionism is a reactionary revolution because the im-
pressionists cease to take cognizance of the semantic character of the work of art. A surface revolution, though not
completely, since content is still retained as important. Impressionism's objects are charmless, modest. Its role is di-
dactic; it functions as a social guide, its task lies in reconciling society to a decline, to the disappearance of a Nature
of the first order or quality. Impressionism continues the
tendency of Occidental art to possess the object through illusion initiated in Greek sculpture and the painting of the
Renaissance. The real problem is to know if the object is signified or reconstituted in a kind of possession—or at least
this is one's aim, since the object is never really reconstituted.

The academicism of impressionism was one of the signified
(or object); the academicism of contemporary art is that of
signifier (or manner). The academicism of language replaces
academicism of subject because no real language is possible,
since this requires social stability and homogeneity. The abstract artist analyzes his own system of signs, dissolving and
exhausting it, voiding it of its signifying function, and of
the very possibility of signifying.[5]

These statements, made by an intellectual hero of our time,
one century after the first Salon des Refusés, ring in my own
ears, and I assume, in yours, with something of a shock, that
shock compounded, of course, by awareness of the culture in
which he was born and came to maturity—that of Paris, a fo-

[4] Claude Lévi-Strauss, *La Pensée Sauvage* (Paris: Librairie Plon, 1962), p. 43.
[5] Ibid., pp. 81-82.

cal center of modernist energies for a century and more. One thinks of Freud, and of his violent rejection of both expressionism and surrealism, his insistence that "the concept of art resisted an extension beyond the point where the quantitative proportion between unconscious material and preconscious elaboration is not kept within a certain limit." [6]

What makes these statements by Lévi-Strauss possible? What do they indicate about the nature of structuralism on the one hand, of our art on the other? Is the conflict real, can we localize it, resolve it? If not, why not? How can a scientific methodology so closely analogous to that of modern aesthetics reject contemporary aesthetic forms?

The source of conflict would seem to lie principally in the application of the linguistic model and of the semantic function to our contemporary painting and sculpture, which resist the notion of any authority or model, any notion of code and message in their stubborn claim for autonomy, immediacy, and absoluteness. To say this is not to deny the manner in which modern art continues to rehearse the contradictions of Platonic idealism, but to recognize that the history of art is, like that of philosophy, a history of ambivalences. The crisis in our notion of the real, initiated in the philosophy of the seventeenth century, inhabits the movement toward abstraction, that movement which rejects the notion of idea or object pre-existent to its aesthetic form, turning from that illusionism through which such objects could be rendered, tending toward the constitution of a more purely pictorial, sculptural, or literary fact. No appreciation of Western art can afford to ignore this, and it has been the strength of American art that its critics and painters have consistently concerned themselves with this crisis and its implications.

This movement, reflected in the development of all the arts, finds an initial affirmation in literature, in a text which stands as a manifesto of modernism, in Flaubert's celebrated letter to Louise Colet, written in January 1852.

[6] This statement appears in a letter written by Freud to Stefan Zweig after a visit from Salvador Dali, published by E. H. Gombrich in "Freud's Aesthetics," *Encounter* (London), January 1966, Vol. XXVI, No. 1.

What I consider fine, what I should like to do, is a book about
nothing, a book without external attachments of any sort,
which would hold of itself, through the inner strength of its
style, as the earth sustains itself with no support in air, a
book with almost no subject. Or at least an almost invisible
subject, if possible.

The dissolution of the subject in the interests of style and
structure was effected through the mediating strategy of the
redefinition of the subject, a leveling of it, the repudiation of
the concept of the "fine" subject, the rehabilitation, the redemp-
tion, through style, of the ordinary. Hence the "modest" quality of impressionist landscapes.

There is an epistemology of modernism that questions the object as it questions the word, thereby questioning the sign.
Art, in questioning mimesis, redefines and loosens its relation
to the signified, aspiring, however, as if by compensation, to
the most radical and most enveloping signification of all, to that
of an absolute presence. Poetry, consenting, through Mallarmé,
to be poetry only, aspires to be "the Orphic explanation of the
world," of a world "meant to end in a book." That book, unwrit-
ten, is prepared for by Mallarmé's supreme effort, *Un Coup de
Dés,* in which the primacy of the work as symbolic sign is questioned at every point of utterance by the felt necessity to make
meaning palpable, as it were, directly perceptible through the
recognition of the space and silence from which it emerges,
which sustain it on the page and in the ear and in the mind.
The word itself, that supreme semantic sign, aspires to a con-
creteness, an immediacy of presence greater than any purely
linguistic concept affords. Henceforth the application of the
classical Saussurian linguistic model will do a certain violence
to art and poetry alike, to their stubborn resistance to meaning
and to their desire to redefine the possibility of meaning
through playfulness and speculation.

Using Peirce's definitions, one could trace the evolution of
painting from the iconic function of Renaissance perspective
to the emergence of the indexical sign in impressionism, its development culminating in the nineteen-forties and fifties as in

Stéphane Mallarmé: Page from *Un Coup de Dés,* 1897

Jackson Pollock or Franz Kline. One sees the play and speculation at work in Jasper Johns' fusion of iconic with indexical, as in his *Targets,* figured and bearing the traces or indices of *facture.* Early works by Robert Morris, involving a plaster cast of a hand, a photograph of the artist, or cardiographs, combine the iconic with the indexical, objectifying process. Lichtenstein has painted in the trajectory of a paintbrush the icon of an index.

No conception of art as language, however, can neglect the manner in which the notion of language itself calls for a certain refinement or extension (the accent on the referent being by no means the only possibility, as Roman Jakobson has pointed out). There do exist messages which perform only the function of establishing, prolonging, or interrupting a circuit

Jasper Johns: *Target with Plaster Casts*, 1955.
Collection Mr. and Mrs. Leo Castelli
(Rudolph Burckhardt photo)

Robert Morris: Untitled, 1963.
Courtesy Leo Castelli Gallery, New York
(Walter Russell photo)

of communication, of attracting attention or insuring that it is not relaxed. This accentuation of contact can give rise to a profusion of ritualistic formulas, or to entire monologues or dialogues whose sole object is to establish or sustain conversation, not to further it. This effort to establish and maintain a communication circuit is characteristic of talking birds, and we call this the phatic function of language, the only one which birds share with us. It is also the first verbal function to be acquired by children. In children, the tendency to establish communication precedes the capacity to emit or receive information-bearing messages. Certain dialogues between critics and artists have that quality.

A year or so ago, while thinking about current art and its resistance to semantic function, I was struck with the manner in which the notion of the "formal statement," a phrase current in contemporary art criticism, represents a vestige of that same tradition which modern criticism proposed to abandon in order to accommodate the intensified immediacy and autonomy of the art object. While rejecting the dualism of code and message and

Roy Lichtenstein: *Little Big Painting*, 1965.
Collection Whitney Museum of American Art, New York, gift of the Friends of the Whitney Museum

confining its concern to an art of a single level of articulation, criticism has, nonetheless, retained something of the old rhetoric. It is that contradiction which gave a certain pungency to John Cage's statement, "I have nothing to say and I am saying it." Art tends increasingly to posit "formal statements" which are positive and nonambiguous, their reductive or nonrelational character resisting denial, debate, and qualification. Statements of this sort we term "apodictic." And the ultimate statement of this kind, the height of immediacy, is reached by the work whose formal statement is merely "I am that I am." The Utopian ideal of this century is, indeed, as Lévi-Strauss has suggested, the construction of a sign system on a single level of articulation. It is the dream of absolute immediacy pervading our culture and our art, which replaces, in a secular age, a theology of absolute presence. That dream is figured on the reverse side of the idealist coin.

Faced with abstraction's single level of articulation, struc-

Robert Morris: Untitled work, 1968. *Courtesy Leo Castelli Gallery, New York (Rudolph Burckhardt photo)*

turalist thinking retreats. (It is significant, by the way, that structuralism has been neither absorbed nor challenged by French art criticism and art history.) Much as Freud turned from expressionism, Lévi-Strauss turns away from the critical view of illusionism and language basic to the epistemology of modernism, and he calls, literally, for the return of an art of imaginary landscapes in *trompe-l'œil*, evoking with Rousseauistic nostalgia the restoration of natural harmony through an art of delectation.

And yet it is, I think, not solely the inapplicability of the linguistic model to modern art, but also the radically rational stance of structuralism that inhibits understanding of the art of our day. The initial Kantian assumption is that "all concepts, even the questions posed in pure reason, reside not in experience, but in reason. . . . Reason it is which engendered these ideas; it is therefore necessary to render account of their value." It follows that only the radical discontinuity between the reality of lived experience and the real as knowable guarantees precision, objectivity, and scientific accuracy. The work of art, however, is that sort of object which is never simply understandable as object, observed, like a foreign cultural pattern, from outside, in a transcendental objectivity, in repudiation of the intentional activity of consciousness. It poses for us, after all, the conditions of experience, of percepton and of apperception, eliciting, within our culture, a response to those perceptions which is cognitive. Our perception of the work of art informs us of the nature of consciousness itself. This is what we mean when we say—as I do say—that, although art no longer means or refers, it does have a deeply cognitive function.

The structural anthropologist, approaching the nonreferent work with the strategies proper to his discipline, ends by treating that work—and, by extension, contemporary art—with the arrogance of a linguistic colonialism, throwing a missionary's mantle of the semantic over the nakedness of art's presence. Garments of this sort are notoriously unbecoming.

It is a curiously paradoxical development, a singular flaw in the exquisite tact and openness which characterize this ethnologist-as-aesthete. The paradox does, however, have a certain logic; or, rather, it tells us that this structuralist's "perspective" on the art of our culture is rooted in the past, in that art of high iconicity which flowered in the rationalized space, through the pictorial perspective of the Renaissance. (Structuralism may have more to say about the richly semantic field of film.)

Criticism and aesthetics, art itself, can no longer proceed without the recognition of continuity between the real as experienced and the real as knowable, of meaning as radically immanent in nonsymbolic signs. They demand that intensive reflexiveness and unsentimental interrogation of our felt experience suspect to Lévi-Strauss, though proposed by the cherished

Albrecht Dürer: *Draftsman Drawing a Lute,* 1525

friend and colleague to whose memory *La Pensée Sauvage* is dedicated.[7] Although that proposal has been slow in reaching our country, its aims and methods and, inevitably, its rhetoric now begin to inform our criticism. The debate between the synchronic and diachronic, between form and history is being drowned in the dialogue between structuralist and phenomenologist, both claiming, of course, the primacy of an ultimate perception.

[7] The phenomenology of Merleau-Ponty "was unsatisfactory to me in so far as it postulated continuity between experience and reality. Although I agree that the latter surrounds and explains the former, I had learned (from the study of geology, Marxism, and psychoanalysis) that the passage from one to another of these two orders is discontinuous; that in order to reach the real we must reject experience, with the possibility of later reintegrating it into an objective synthesis stripped of all sentimentality." Claude Lévi-Strauss, *Tristes Tropiques* (Paris: Librairie Plon, 1955), pp. 44-45.

Creating the
Creative Artist

B. F. SKINNER

*B. F. Skinner is Edgar Pierce Professor of Psychology at
Harvard University and the author of several important
books on behavioral psychology and teaching techniques, as
well as of the controversial Utopian novel* Walden Two.

There are many reasons why we may want to give art a more
important place in our culture. Perhaps we simply want more
art available to be enjoyed. Perhaps we believe that a culture
in which art flourishes is stronger because it attracts and holds
people who can solve practical problems. But our reasons, whatever they may be, are by no means as important as our pros-
pects. What can be done to further the production and consumption of art?

Art and Leisure

A relation between art and leisure has long been recognized.
Early man had to free himself from a constant preoccupation
with food, shelter, and safety before he could begin to decorate
his clothing, his dwelling, his weapons, and his body and eventually create things with no other function than to be decora-
tive. When civilizations reach the stage at which many people
enjoy leisure, great periods of art often begin. We acknowledge the connection when we encourage artists by giving them
leisure—through patronage, fellowships, grants, or sinecures.

The archetypal connection between art and bohemianism or between art and life in a garret is in the same pattern, for these are devices through which the artist gives himself leisure, by avoiding commitments and living cheaply.

The relation is easily misunderstood. Certainly not everyone becomes an artist as soon as he is free to do so. And the artist will be the first to insist that just because he has managed to dispose of the things we say he "has" to do, he is not in any real sense free. The serious, dedicated artist must do what he does as earnestly and as compellingly as other men struggle for food, shelter, or safety. The difference is merely in the conspicuousness of the causes. We usually know why people behave as they do when they "have" to do so, but less powerful reasons are usually less obvious. They exist, however, and if we are going to encourage people to be artists (or, for that matter, consumers of art), we ought to know what they are.

The Reasons for Art

Why, indeed, do artists paint? The traditional answers are not very helpful. They refer to events supposedly taking place inside the artist himself. The artist who has been freed from the pressures of the world around him is said to be able to express his individuality, his creative impulses, his love of beauty, the agony and ecstasy of his inner struggles. These are engaging theories. They represent the artist as a complex person living a dramatic life, and they give him exclusive credit for the beautiful things he creates. But we have not really explained the artist's achievement in terms of his inner life if we have learned about that life only from his achievements.

It is true that artists talk about themselves and very often about their inner lives. They are no doubt in an excellent position to observe the behavior of artists, but we must accept their accounts with caution. When they talk about their emotions, thoughts, ideas, and impulses, they necessarily use a vocabulary that has been taught to them by people who have had no contact with these things and who, therefore, cannot teach them to describe them accurately. As a result every artist gives his own idiosyncratic account, and his answer to the question "Why does the artist paint as he does?" is probably no more helpful than that of anyone else.

Nor does the traditional view help us in furthering the production and enjoyment of art. We have no direct contact with the mind or emotions of the artist. Only indirectly, if at all, can we induce him to have strong feelings or original ideas. If art springs from an inner life which is truly original, in the sense that it *begins* with the artist, then there is nothing to be done beyond giving the artist an opportunity. It is much more promising, however, to argue that the achievements of the artist can be traced to the world in which he lives, for we can then begin to examine that world, not only to explain the achievements, but to find the means of taking practical steps.

The colloquial "What for?" is often a useful synonym for "Why?" What do artists make paintings *for?* What do people look at paintings *for?* The term points to the future and emphasizes an important fact. Artists paint *because of the consequences*, and people look at paintings *because of the consequences*. In traditional terms, the consequences may be said to define the purposes of art, but there is a more important implication. The relation between behavior and its consequences has recently been studied in considerable detail. In hundreds of laboratories throughout the world, in a special scientific discipline called the experimental analysis of behavior, various kinds of consequences are made contingent upon behavior in complex ways, and the effect on the probability that an organism will behave in a given way is observed. Certain kinds of consequences are said to "reinforce" behavior in the sense that they make it more likely to occur. We need not go into details here, but if we can discover the "reinforcers" which are contingent upon the artist's behavior when he makes a painting, and upon the behavior of others when they look at paintings, we can not only explain the behavior but use our knowledge to give art a more important role in our culture.

The word "reinforcing," though technical, is useful as a

rough synonym for "interesting," "attractive," "pleasing," and "satisfying," and all these terms are commonly applied to paintings. For our present purposes it is particularly useful as a synonym for "beautiful." Paintings are by definition reinforcing in the sense that they are responsible for the fact that artists paint them and people look at them. It is a mistake to suppose that they do this because of how people feel about them. Feelings are mere by-products; the important thing is what a painting does to behavior. The artist puts paint on canvas and is or is not reinforced by the result. If he is reinforced, he goes on painting. Others look at the painting and are or are not reinforced for doing so. If they are reinforced, they continue to look and to seek other works to look at.

To some extent we are reinforced by works of art for idiosyncratic reasons. Consumers of art have different preferences, and so have artists. The integrity of an artist's work is in part a matter of what features have reinforced him. If he is unduly reinforced when his paintings sell, he may begin to make paintings which are likely to sell. The reinforcing effect of a painting is, however, significant for another reason.

The Competitors of Art

Let us look again at the relation between art and leisure. Things we "have to do" are under the control of powerful reinforcers. When hungry, we are dominated by behavior which has been reinforced by food. When under a threat, we are absorbed in avoidance or escape. But when free of powerful reinforcers, *we are simply more vulnerable to weak ones*. Leisure brings the artist under the control of inconspicuous reinforcers.

But works of art are not the only reinforcers which take over when serious consequences have been eliminated. Members of the leisure class are not all artists. On the contrary, the leisure to be observed in either an affluent society or a welfare state has a variety of quite different effects. It may lead, for example, to play—to behavior resembling serious behavior but exhibited for less than serious reasons (as in hunting and fishing when what is caught, captured, or killed is not eaten) or to playing games in which trivial consequences have been made critical (will the ball fall into the hole?). Gambling is characteristic of leisure, and all gambling systems are designed to make consequences particularly effective by making them contingent on behavior in unpredictable ways. Sexual behavior is characteristic of leisure because it is concerned with the survival of the species rather than the individual and is not subject to more efficient satiation through technological advances. Synthetic reinforcers, such as alcohol or marijuana, are among the nonessentials which take over in leisure. Spectatorship is a common feature, and recent technological advances have made it possible for vast numbers of people to watch others engage in the serious business of life, undergoing crucial personal experiences in drama, being hurt in football and other games, or undergoing the risks of exploration in space.

These are the natural competitors of art. How can we give art a chance against them? If art needs leisure, leisure needs art. In essence, how can we induce the artist to paint more pictures, and everyone else to look at them? The obvious answer is this: Make sure that painting and looking are abundantly reinforced. And here we see the advantage in substituting "reinforcing" for "beautiful." No matter what other aspects of beauty the critic may wish to emphasize, we are for the moment interested simply in the reinforcing effect of a painting. What is it about a painting that makes the artist more inclined to continue painting it and the viewer to look at it and continue to do so?

Why a Painting Is Reinforcing

From time to time answers have been sought in paintings themselves. Beauty, it has been said, is in the object, and we have only to analyze a large number of beautiful objects to discover it. But different people in different ages and in dif-

ferent cultures have found different things beautiful, and if
there are indeed objective properties which make a thing
beautiful or reinforcing, they must be less important than
other reasons.

We say that a painting is reinforcing because of its content,
but this is not a full explanation of why we look at it. It is
reinforcing because it resembles real things, but these are
reinforcing for other reasons. An exhaustive account would
explain all of human behavior as well. Contingencies of survival
in the evolution of the human race have made the human form
an important visual reinforcer, and the human figure is, of
course, a common subject matter in the art of many cultures.
Foodstuffs become reinforcing for other biological reasons,
and it should occasion no surprise that people have, from time
to time, hung pictures of fruit, fish, and game in their dining
rooms. Portraits of people we love or admire permit us to look
at the people when they are absent, and when the young lover
kisses the portrait of his beloved he is only exemplifying in a
conspicuous way the kind of thing we all do when we look at a
portrait: we behave toward the portrait to some slight extent
as we should behave toward the person portrayed. The artist
who relies mainly on content to make his paintings reinforcing
is usually held deficient in other respects.

We turn from content to abstract form in a search for other
kinds of reinforcing things which are less obviously traceable
to the history of the individual or species. But we must not forget that what we *do* about an abstraction is still the important
thing. Denman Ross pointed this out in 1907 in his *Theory of
Pure Design*—a book which, though not particularly influential, could be regarded as the manifesto of abstractionism. A
design induces the viewer to look at it, and in a way which is
common to so many visual presentations that we divorce it from
content altogether and regard it as possibly close to an essential artistic process. But if an abstract picture induces a
painter to finish painting it and viewers to look at it, it is because it has reinforcing properties. (The loss of content is
to some extent a loss of power, and some contemporary artists

offset this with a use of abstract material which is as exaggerated as the most maudlin sentimentality in representational art.)

Other issues commonly encountered in discussions of art can be restated in terms of reinforcement. The history of art is to a large extent the history of what artists and viewers have found reinforcing. Universality is the universality of reinforcing effects. Changes in fashion come about as some reinforcers lose power and others gain. The emphasis is important in its bearing upon the practical problem of improving the place of art in a culture.

There is not much the nonartist can do to make art itself more reinforcing. That is the artist's own field, and it must be left to him. It is he who must discover new kinds of reinforcers in the sense of new forms of beauty. But there are other things to be done. There are ways in which the nonartist can make it more likely that the artist will be reinforced by the works that he makes. To become an artist (or, in the course of a career, to become a different kind of artist) is a form of learning. The "instruction" responsible for it may be entirely accidental. Can it be deliberate? Can we teach a person to be an artist? So far as technique goes, the answer is yes. And that fact is relevant to the present issue. The more competent the artist, the more reinforcing his work is likely to be—other things being equal. But what about the "other things"? Can we actually teach an artist how to discover or invent new forms of beauty in the sense of new kinds of reinforcers?

The easy answer is no, and it is usually given by those who continue to regard artistic achievement as the expression of an inner life. Such a life is not directly within reach of a teacher; genius must be left to work its way out. And if that is the nature of art, then, apart from technique, the teacher cannot teach but only help the artist learn. Moreover, he must think twice about teaching technique, lest he interfere with untaught creative expression. The position has the support of many educational philosophies outside the field of art, where subject matter is abandoned in order to strengthen an inquiring spirit. The position is in essence a renunciation of teaching: the student is somehow better off if he is left to discover things himself.

The "discovery method" is particularly attractive to those who are interested in producing original artists, but we should first be sure that it works. It is by definition not a method of instruction at all. It arose, in fact, from a concern with motivation. When teachers abandoned older forms of discipline, they lost control, and to the extent that they have not found suitable substitutes, it is quite correct to say that they can no longer teach. And they have, therefore, been tempted to let students discover knowledge for themselves.

But we do not need to abandon subject matter in order to teach discovery. It is not true that if we fill the student's head with facts he will be unable to think for himself. He is not damaged by facts but only by the ways in which facts have been taught. There is no reason why methods of discovery must be taught by the discovery method. Learning the techniques of others does not interfere with the discovery of techniques of one's own. On the contrary, the artist who has acquired a variety of techniques from his predecessors is in the best possible position to make truly original discoveries. And he is most likely to be original if he has been taught how to be so.

The very assignment of producing a *creative* artist may seem contradictory. How can behavior be original or creative if it has been "produced"? Production presupposes some form of external control, but creativity, taken literally, denies such control. That is why we tend to associate it with an inner life. Arthur Koestler has taken this line in his book *The Act of Creation.* For Koestler, a behavioral analysis of creativity is not only impossible but ludicrous, since novelty cannot arise in a "mechanistic" system. A creative *mind* must be at work. But "a creative mind" explains nothing. It is an appeal to the miraculous: mind is brought in to do what the body cannot do. But we must then explain how the mind does it, and when we approach that assignment we discover that we must still answer all our original questions but that they are now stated in a more difficult, if not an impossible, form.

Novelty or originality can occur in a wholly deterministic system. A convenient archetypal pattern is the theory of evolution. The living forms on the earth show a variety far beyond that of works of art. The diversity was once attributed to the whims and vagaries of a creative Mind, but Darwin proposed an alternative explanation. The word "origin" in *The Origin of Species* is important, for the book is essentially a study of originality. The multiplicity of living forms is accounted for in terms of mutation and selection, without appealing to any prior design. There are comparable elements in the behavior of the artist who produces original works.

The artist facing a clean canvas is in much the same position as the writer facing a clean sheet of paper. What is to be put on it, and where is it to come from? (Those who insist that artists, like writers, must first have ideas must rephrase the question accordingly: What ideas are to be put on the clean slate of the mind, and where do they come from?) There are some simple answers. If the artist has already successfully put paint on canvas, he is likely to do the same thing again. If he has learned to copy things which are reinforcing, he can convert his clean canvas into a reinforcing object by copying something which has proved reinforcing elsewhere. It is tempting, of course, to copy other pictures, but when the other pictures have been painted by other artists, the copies will be the source of little satisfaction or approval. Artists are permitted, however, to copy themselves. Only the first Picasso was not derivative: all the others were derivative of earlier Picassos.

What we call an original or creative painting must come from other sources. We must look for "mutations." Many of these are accidental in the sense that they arise from conditions which we cannot now identify in the genetic and environmental histories of the artist and from unpredictable details of his working methods and conditions. We may not like to credit any aspect of a successful painting to chance, but if we are willing to admit that chance does make a contribution, we can take steps to improve the chances. Mutations may be made more probable by making the control of a medium less precise or by encouraging disturbances. In the Second World War new types of electronic equipment were used which could not be made wholly reliable in the available time, and an element was therefore sometimes introduced to keep the equipment in constant vibration. If a relay stuck, it would be instantly shaken loose. The vibration was called "dither." The artist introduces a source of dither when he adds an extra length of handle to his brush, or paints with bits of sponge instead of a brush, or pours paint on a horizontal canvas. He can generate mutations by changing his working conditions, by working when he is tired, cold, discouraged, or drunk. He can generate other kinds of mutations by deliberately doing what he has been taught not to do; he can violate standards, conventions, and taboos, as a mathematician denies self-evident axioms or a composer uses previously forbidden harmonies. Randomness is most obviously deliberate when the artist spins a dial, throws dice, or consults a table of random numbers and puts paint on canvas as the results dictate.

Mutation must, however, be followed by selection. Not every product of carelessness, a cold studio, the deliberate rejection of a convention, or the roll of dice is a work of art. Putting paint on canvas is no more important than letting it stand, changing it, or scraping it off. The painting eventually left on the canvas is only one product of the combined process of mutation and selection. An artist who will henceforth paint in a different way is another. The selective side of the artist's role emphasizes his uniqueness and the almost infinite variety of the circumstances under which he lives and paints. But selection is also learned and can presumably be taught. The young artist may be taught, for example, to tolerate effects he once rejected, to permit some features to stand for the sake of others, to stop painting in time, and so on.

The Role of the Consumer

Apart from the idiosyncratic factors which play a part in mutation and selection, an artist is to some extent reinforced when others enjoy his work. We can help by making sure that his work will be enjoyed. We should be explicit about this. We are to induce more people to look at more paintings and for longer periods of time—to seek out paintings to look at, as by going to museums, and to buy paintings in order that they may be looked at. People do all this when paintings are reinforcing. How can they be made so?

The artist himself is concerned with producing consumers. Whether or not he paints primarily because of effects upon himself, he makes works of art which are reinforcing to others when they look at them. As nonartists we can help. We want paintings to be more valuable to those who look at them, in the sense of more effective in inducing them to continue to look. That is one of the functions of art education: people are taught to look at paintings in ways which are more likely to be reinforced. "Art appreciation" is an apt expression, for it is a matter of increasing the reinforcing value of art, and it is appropriate to use the same term as in speaking of an appreciation in price.

We can scarcely be proud of what is now being done, however. Only a small part of the average school curriculum is devoted to the enjoyment of art—or, for that matter, to the enjoyment of music or literature. It is the misfortune of all three fields to be taught as mysteries, to which effective methods of instruction are held not to apply. Very little beyond simple communication and conspicuous enjoyment is attempted. The emphasis is on the feelings engendered by books, music, and pictures. Students may not read books, listen to music, or look at pictures without feelings, but an increased likelihood that they will do these things is the goal of education.

An important opportunity to encourage creative art by

multiplying consumers is often overlooked. A comparison with music is instructive. A generation or two ago very few people could hear good music. For everyone who heard a symphony orchestra or opera, thousands got no farther than the brass band on the village green or the parlor piano. The phonograph and radio made a prodigious difference. Vast numbers of people now hear music of unlimited variety and excellent quality. A recorded performance is often better than an actual symphony heard from many of the seats in a symphony hall. If there is not yet a golden age in musical composition, the stage is certainly set for one. As Roy Harris has said, the long-playing record "is to music what the printing press was to literature." There is nothing like it yet in the field of art. Those who are engaged in reproducing pictures lack the power and zeal of the electronics industry. Most copies of paintings are fragile, awkward to handle, and hard to store or display. Fidelity is generally low. How little attention is paid to this is evident in the fact that new issues of reproductions are not reviewed in the popular press, as new records are.

What is needed, however, is not only better reproductions but also a basic change in attitude. Copies of works of art are suspect. No one is bothered by the fact that a good phonograph is not actually an orchestra, but many people are bothered by the fact that a painting is not genuine. A very good copy, indeed, suggests a forgery. Another difficulty is that people seldom change the paintings on their walls. Paintings are regarded as part of the decoration of a room, or they are permanently displayed as valuable possessions. They then either cease to be noticed or become as objectionable as background music. (It may be argued that one need not look at a painting and one cannot help listening to music, but background music is not always heard.) Paintings should be enjoyed as music is enjoyed, and they should be as easily "played."

Dedication

The proper reinforcement of artistic behavior can have another important effect. Life is greater than art, and both producer and consumer of art are, as we have seen, under the control of relatively weak reinforcers. But it is significant that the natural competitors of art are also weakly reinforced. Far more people visit race tracks than museums, buy lottery tickets than paintings, and look at televised football games than paintings, but the competing *reinforcers* are not actually stronger. The net reinforcement at the race track or in a lottery is indeed almost always negative (the gambler eventually loses), and the victory of a favorite team could scarcely be less important in itself. Something has *made* these reinforcers effective, and, thanks to recent research, we know what it is. A weak reinforcer exerts a powerful control when effectively scheduled. All gambling systems and all games and sports "pay off" in a special unpredictable way. The behavior of placing a bet or playing a game is reinforced on a so-called "variable-ratio" schedule, and the schedule generates a high level of activity. On such schedules pigeons as well as men become pathological gamblers. We can create "pathological" artists and viewers of art with the same system.

A person who, as we say, lives for art, for whom art is the most important thing in the world, is not so much one who finds art reinforcing as one who has enjoyed a favorable history of painting or looking at pictures. The technique with which a dishonest gambler "hooks" his victim shows what needs to be done. The first reinforcements must be quick and easy, but the average amount of behavior demanded for each reinforcement must then slowly increase. Eventually the behavior is maintained for long periods of time, possibly without any reinforcement whatsoever. Instruction in the enjoyment of art should begin with arrangements in which reinforcement is generous, and perhaps "cheap." Even the meretricious may have its place. More difficult ("better") materials should be introduced with care as instruction proceeds. It is often hard to arrange effective programs, but the teacher must not neglect the possibility of doing so. The dedicated artist, like the dedicated hunter, fisherman, explorer, or scientist, is the product of a probably accidental but happy program of successes. An effective program may arise naturally as an artist strives for more and more difficult effects or a viewer turns to reinforcing features of a picture which are to be found less and less often.

Philistinism?

We have considered only some of the more obvious reasons why people paint and look at pictures. We have scarcely touched on the many different kinds of things to be found in paintings or the effects they have on artist or viewer. (We have not, of course, considered forms of art other than painting.) We have not traced the effects of paintings on personal histories. It is easy, therefore, to say that the account is oversimplified. But the central point deserves consideration. People paint and look at pictures for good reasons—which can be investigated. Prominent among the reasons are certain reinforcing consequences, and recent advances in the experimental analysis of behavior have shown their importance. There is a practical implication: when consequences can be manipulated, behavior can be changed. Technological applications are already well advanced in other fields. Why should we not use this knowledge to induce more people to take an interest in art?

Perhaps it is a kind of philistinism to suppose that we can "produce" artists, as if they were some sort of commodity. Certainly the position is incompatible with many traditional conceptions. But is it unrealistic? Art is produced by a culture or a mixture of cultures. People commonly act to change the culture in which they live, and they do so in order to change its effects. We change our culture in an effort to further art when we subsidize artists, teach or encourage the teaching of art, make works of art more generally available, and so on, and some of these measures can now be greatly improved. Even so, they will affect only a small part of the conditions responsible for any artist, let alone any great artist. We have no specific control over these conditions, but we make them more likely to occur. The occasional chess genius is most likely to appear in a culture in which many people play chess, and a great artist is most likely to arise when the production and consumption of art are important parts of a way of life.

If we are willing to accept the assignment of making our culture more effective in this way, then we should turn to a formulation of human behavior which points to things to be done. Traditional explanations have seldom led to effective action; they are supported primarily by the weight of tradition and the fascination of the inexplicable. Perhaps nothing less than a resolute philistinism will permit us to build the background from which, for reasons we admit we do not fully understand, more creative artists will emerge.[1]

[1] Many of the points in this lecture are discussed in detail in the author's *Science and Human Behavior* (New York: Macmillan, 1963) and *The Technology of Teaching* (New York: Appleton-Century-Crofts, 1968.) Preparation of this paper has been supported in part by a Career Award by the National Institutes of Mental Health (grant K6-MH-21, 775-01).

Phenomenal Art:
Form, Idea, and Technique

JAMES SEAWRIGHT

Mr. Seawright is a sculptor working in New York City, where he is affiliated with the Columbia-Princeton Electronic Music Center. He has taught at Princeton University and the School of Visual Arts in New York City, and his works are in several museums and private collections throughout the United States.

I'd like to talk about certain aspects of the kind of work I do. It's a kind of work a number of other people are doing too, and one which I believe will sooner or later become predominant in the concerns of artists. I will try to substantiate such a rash claim as I go on, but first I would like to clear up something about the "phenomenal art" of my title. I use the term to describe, in an approximate way, works that undergo actual change with the passage of time. I want you, however, to eliminate from consideration works that produce phenomena which are the result of some change in the relationship between the work and the viewer: changes of perspective, visual illusions, that sort of thing. What I want to talk about are sculptures or objects or systems—whatever you want to call them—that undergo changes of their own, active changes, in time, changes that are inherent in them, that they were constructed to produce physically. These changes, or phenomena, might be changes of illumination, of spatial relationships, or of sound production. I don't wish to suggest that there is any philosophical notion of phenomenalism involved, nor do I think that any particular aesthetic attitude is necessary in order to consider this type of work from the point of view of the artist. As far as I'm concerned, my own works produce phenomena actively, and I am interested in the form and structure in which these phenomena are organized, the origin of the ideas that underlie the phenomena, and the methods of producing and controlling the phenomena.

Let us consider a structure that incorporates real lamps. To whatever physical properties the structure may have must be added the properties of the phenomena produced by turning the lights on or off, individually or in groups, in some temporal sequence. The lamps may be controlled in a binary fashion— that is to say, they may be either "on" or "off"—or they may exhibit intermediate levels of brightness. Conceivably, the color of the light can be controlled as well, although this is not easily done in practice. I think it is possible to make an analogy between the totality of the phenomena produced by this structure of lamps and, let's say, a piece of music, or the performance of a piece of music. You can, of course, carry the analogy too far. A sculptor who builds a device producing some kind of time-dependent phenomenon is probably going to solve the problems related to it in a way entirely different from the way a composer of music would use, because he will more likely be using mechanical means to control the lamps or whatever the parts are that produce the phenomena. I wouldn't rule out the *possibility* of having an "orchestra" or a group of people operating some kind of phenomena-producing device, but it would never occur to me to use this method in the majority of cases, because of the easy availability of a mechanism to do the job. More significant than the use of mechanisms to control phenomena is the fact that one can take advantage of the mechanism's ability to control itself; in other words, one can use automatic or self-regulating mechanisms, which have properties both very like and very unlike what human beings consider to be organization and order.

Let's suppose that we want to compose a pattern of

phenomena, such as a series of light changes. If we have a mechanism to produce them, or if we have to construct one, we must be able to describe what we want in some kind of language intelligible to the mechanism. This requires a consideration of the result we want in a way not generally experienced by artists heretofore. A good example of this is found in music. Composers today usually represent a score by means of symbols, each one of which carries a tremendous amount of information. Through the evolution of music there has been a tendency to think of the notation of a musical event in a score as an adequate representation of the actual event, but this is not true unless you can rely on the performer's understanding of all the implications of the symbol and of the ways his body and instrument will behave when he attempts to carry out the action called for by the symbol. When you produce a piece of electronic music, you no longer have the performer's experience and skill to help in interpreting the real meaning of the symbolic instructions, and you must cause the electronic equipment to reproduce your exact intentions by giving instructions even down to the most absurd detail. If the particular things you want done are extremely complex or full of nuance, and thereby difficult to explain in every detail, it might be preferable to produce works of art in which phenomena other than sounds (or in addition to sounds) are the content of the work and in which these phenomena are produced under the control of other people. You would then be able to utilize the individual judgment of these persons who are in control, and this might be in effect an extension of your own taste.

But let us say that you do use a mechanism to produce a series of phenomena. Once you learn how to make the mechanism and how to shape information into a form it can understand or embody, you will see that there is a certain equivalency between the body of information you put into the mechanism as a program of instruction and the totality of the phenomena produced. This equivalency, simply a transformation of one kind of information into another, suggests the possibility of using bodies of information which already exist. Rather than

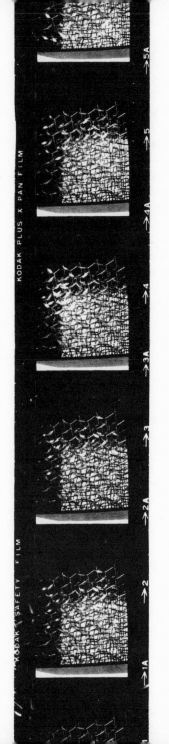

Photocrystal II, 1965.
Collection of the artist

try to compose in advance every detail of the performance you want to have, you might be able to find a "bulk" form or a "bulk" kind of performance (that is, a body of information already possessing some degree of organization) and then attempt to change its structure and to reorganize or modify its instructions into suitable material for performance.

Now let's look at a specific example—several shots of a piece, *Photocrystal II,* taken at random, showing whatever it happened to be doing at the moment. Here, the phenomena of the lights going on and off represent the direct transformation of the movements of a mechanism into the motions and patterns of the lights. The pattern of movements is cyclical, but it takes twelve hours or so to go through the whole cycle. Within the cycle, there's a dynamic variation in what it does; there's a pattern in the rate at which activity follows inactivity. It seems to me that one of the crucial issues involved in working in a medium where the passage of time is significant is that you are obligated to exert some kind of control. Whether you're aware of it or not, whether you decide to let the lamps be switched on and off at random, let them all be on, or let them all be off, you have to make some decision about it. Even if you don't care—that in itself is a decision. In view of the possible ways that it can be done, this example represents one approach.

A kind of sacrifice is involved in controlling the totality of the phenomena produced, because if you start with a mechanism that has certain properties and you begin to tamper with one part of it by changing the length of a linkage or the number of teeth on a gear, you affect the whole cycle to some degree, however effectively you change the particular aspect you set out to change. This ability to shape or modify the "character" or behavior of one mechanism can be increased by compounding or bringing together several self-sufficient information-transforming mechanisms to produce or control the phenomena of a single work. There's also a secondary effect which I think is noteworthy: I was quite surprised to find at first that the mechanisms responsible for producing the phenomena were

Watcher, 1965. Collection Howard and Jean Lipman (Schiff photo)

in some ways more interesting visually than the phenomena themselves—the kinetic, the sheer kinetic behavior of them, the linkages going all over the place. This, I think, is an illustration of the fact that you can't simply come from the outside with an idea and try to apply it by bending the technological resources that you may have (or can acquire) to suit it. The more I work, the more I believe that the best ideas grow out of an understanding of the processes being used, rather than out of a preconceived notion of the effects to be achieved.

The next example, *Watcher,* is a piece in which a deliberate effort was made to use several different, independent programed mechanisms whose information content is directly transformed into phenomena. The actual mechanisms are all fully visible and contribute to the total visual effect. There's at least one relationship or subsystem in the work in which sensors detect or receive information which constitutes one set of phenomena, and transform it into still another form, another set of phenomena. This amounts to a transformation of the light phenomena into electronically generated sounds, which originate in the structure in the left-hand part of the illustration. The information required to specify the characteristics of the sounds is received by the photocells which scan the bank of lamps. You certainly have no way of predicting, in a practical way, where they are going to be pointing at any given time—if you bend one photocell a little bit too much, it sees another lamp, and so forth—but it's quite interesting to note how well the character of the sound seems to correspond to and enhance the idea of cause and effect.

I'd like to go back now and reiterate one or two things. I very much want to get across my thought that the interrelationship between form, idea, and the techniques used applies in a special way to this kind of work. I certainly can see that this is a statement one has always been able to make about various kinds of art, but in time-dependent work, where the concern is primarily with the phenomena themselves, it's almost inevitable that the forms evolved for treating these phenomena, whether organizing them or structuring them, will be analogous to the forms that have evolved in a much older performing art, such as music. The necessity of organizing in a cyclical way certainly takes away some element of development, some element of drama, perhaps, in beginning with something and building into something else, so that it is very hard to say where form stops and idea begins.

There are other factors involved, which also represent compromises. Once you decide to define something, to limit it, to package it—once you say, "All right, I'm going to make something that works and is a sculpture, and I'll put it in a gallery, and people will look at it"—you can no longer legitimately say, "Well, I don't really care what people think about it; I simply made it because I wanted to, and that's that." You really have to consider what people think, because you run into the most incredible spectrum of reactions from people, which seems to arise out of the ambiguous position the object occupies in their experience. Once you allow work to be shown that, in addition to affecting viewers in the way works of art usually do, is able to capture and engage their attention by performing, you are more or less committed—at least this is my feeling—to making the process as efficient as possible. Thus, when you get reactions like "How does it work?" or "To what extent is it necessary to know how it works?" or even "What is it?" you realize that something is getting in the way of their simply regarding the work. I don't feel that my pieces are just demonstrations of complicated processes, techniques that you have to know about, and so forth, but in any case I can't really judge this, because I *do* know how they work. And I feel that the ideas themselves and the way they are presented have grown out of knowing, or at least thinking about, the processes or the techniques that interested me at the time.

The next piece, *Tetra,* is an even better example of what I'm talking about. To describe it physically: it stands about seven feet tall; the hublike thing is actually a cluster of four little motors with large spoked wheels attached to them, arranged symmetrically as the vertices of a tetrahedron; the whole thing

Tetra, 1966. *Brandeis University Art Collection, gift of*
Mrs. Frederick Hilles, New Haven, Conn. (Schiff photo)

is supported on a rod from the triangular base. This piece uses little motors that are called "selsyns." These selsyns have the property of turning clockwise or counterclockwise a certain amount in order to remain exactly in step with other selsyns, to which they are connected electrically. They are used as remote indicators or as a means of transmitting a motion without an actual mechanical connection. Because, as in any electric motor, the force that operates them is a magnetic attraction between their fixed and moving parts, the selsyns have a certain elasticity. For instance, when rotors, or wheels having rotational inertia, are attached to the shafts of the selsyns, the rotation of one wheel will not produce an instantaneous response in the others, but will set up a condition in which a restoring force tries to bring them back into alignment.

This piece grew out of experiments with the little selsyns. The reason four were used is that four was the largest number that seemed to work reasonably well before the effects grew too weak (the selsyns were originally designed to be used only in pairs). The questions of the geometrical organization of the piece are obviously related to the use of four selsyns. The spoked wheels in the piece were determined by the nature of the selsyns that turn them. For these selsyns the wheels can't be too heavy; a spoked wheel gives the appearance of being quite large without being too heavy. So far, so good. If you turn one wheel with a breath of air or a touch, the other three try to follow, but because of their inertia they swing back and forth as they try to get back in alignment, and a kind of oscillation takes place before they finally reach equilibrium again.

When the piece reached this stage, I began to run into artifacts, or consequences, of the process involved. For instance, these little selsyns were originally intended to be used in aircraft, and in order for them to be small and light, they were designed to use 400-cycle AC power instead of the normal 60 cycles. So I had to build a 400-cycle power supply. The kind of 400-cycle power supply that is cheapest and simplest to build is stable only if the power demand on it is constant. But when the wheels were turned and the selsyns were put out of align-ment, that is, when the restoring force or tension was created, the power demand increased, and the frequency of the power supply increased. This happened to be clearly audible as a sound, because of slight vibrations of all the mechanical parts. So you see, all kinds of things which I certainly could not have anticipated appeared at every step. And I had to decide whether to go with it or fight against it. The spokes could have been made longer in order to resonate the sound better. But suppose the pitch of the sound had not increased when there was a tension, and had gone down instead? What do any of these things mean in perceptual terms?

I'm not going into all of this to extol the virtues of the piece. That's totally beside the point. The point is that the problem of making the piece work, of making it function in some active way, necessarily involves you in an area of concepts that I think is central to our times, and that is technology. There's a difference between the understanding of a technological process and the understanding of anything else, I think. Perhaps it's just that technology *can* be understood. I believe that artists will be simply unable to resist the power that the medium seems to offer, once they are working with it or become more exposed to it. For instance, to go back once again to the illustration, my feeling about the piece is that, in a very rudimentary or primi-tive way, it possesses an actual *sensitivity.* If you do something to it, it reacts. Reactivity. It possesses a behavior. It possesses an unpredictability. And yet it's just nuts and bolts. In order to reconcile this somehow, I think you have to recognize that technology is offering us the power to animate things, literally, and the opportunity to intensify or amplify the intention to signify animate phenomena that has always existed with artists. This is an irresistible power indeed.

Let me show you another example. This is another kind of development; it goes beyond the last piece in that an effort was made here to construct a kind of automaton. The piece, *Searcher,* either seeks or avoids light, depending on the state

Searcher, 1966. Collection Whitney Museum of American Art,
New York, gift of Howard and Jean Lipman Foundation, Inc.
(Schiff photo)

of internal circuits, and the changes which occur in its circuits constitute a program. There is, however, an unpredictability involved, since it's a powerful source of light itself and will be either frustrating or encouraging its own efforts to react to light. This behavior is susceptible to modification according to the way in which the piece is adjusted. The wide variations in the over-all pattern of behavior which this piece will exhibit in a room full of people, at night, or in bright daylight make it clear that environmental influences are strong. When a person walks in front of it, and it happens to be in a certain state (of internal connection), it will follow that person around the room with its light beam. It's impossible not to think that this isn't what it's "supposed to do" except that it will ignore him the next time, even if he tries to induce an expected reaction by some provocative movement. But now his reaction to the piece is beginning to color the relationship between it and himself. This kind of encounter isn't really as theatrical as it sounds, because the artist has much less control. But as the artist, you are setting up a generalized set of options and throwing them, so to speak, at an audience. What you observe, you try to refine for the next piece.

I was interested in carrying this still further. The two pieces *Captive* and *Scanner* are both basically the same as *Searcher*. They operate exactly the same way but they have completely different configurations, and when I had all three together for the first time in the same room, it became quite obvious that, whether there were people around or not, there was plenty of interaction between the pieces. And I thought that was very entertaining: an environment of interaction in which it was possible to participate without dominating.

I would like to conclude by talking about the latest thing I have done. This is an environment-piece which I was commissioned to design for the Kansas City Performing Arts Foundation. It was called *Electronic Peristyle*. It consists of a circle twenty-one feet across, bordered by columns; within this space there is a false floor with the supporting structures underneath. In the center is a control unit. The idea was to bring the viewer

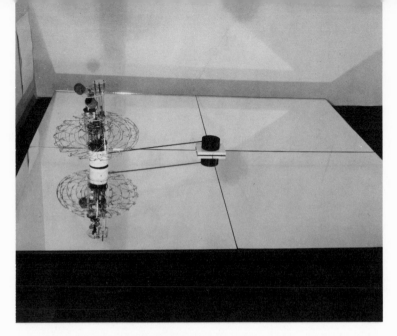

Captive, 1966. Collection Aldrich Museum of Contemporary Art, Ridgefield, Conn. (Schiff photo)

Scanner, 1966. Courtesy Stable Gallery, New York (Schiff photo)

into the thing, isolating external influences and, as far as possible, letting only the actual movements of the viewer be the information transformed and used to generate the phenomena. The phenomena were patterns of sound, light, and wind emanating from the columns.

A person can enter the circle, and his movements will be detected and recorded in the center unit as patterns of data in digital form. The center unit functions as a limited kind of computer, performing certain operations with the data as program steps and then decoding the data into electronically generated sounds and light patterns and, occasionally, wind effects. The way the effects, or phenomena, are organized is designed to allow the viewer to see that he is influencing what is going on, although it is initially unclear just how he can anticipate what effect his actions will have. The longer he is involved, however, the more he is able to see what he is controlling and what he isn't. The pictures give you some idea of the appearance of the environment, although the lighting is unnaturally bright, owing to the necessity of photographing it; actually the piece is quite dark inside.

The piece is really a very, very crude approach to what I think it is possible to do. The piece observes the viewer in a very simple way: it detects whether he passes one of a number of points. It determines practically nothing about his reactions and presents him with very limited inducements for continued interest. But the possibilities for development and refinement are almost unlimited, for the quantity of information that can be managed in this type of arrangement is quite staggering, and yet it isn't really a very expensive proposition. It is, moreover, something that was practically impossible a few years ago.

I believe, however, that there may be a limit as to how far one can go in a quasi-theatrical direction. The more people that get in this sort of piece, the less chance there is for any comprehension of the phenomena as they relate to the individual viewer in the framework of the system. It really works best with only one person. If there are two people in there, they have to cooperate, or else they become simply adversaries.

Electronic Peristyle, 1968. *Courtesy Kansas City Performing Arts Foundation (Ross Taggart photo)*

Electronic Peristyle

While working with a number of people has some interesting possibilities for future pieces, it just leads to problems in this one, and I don't see any practical way to solve them. It's as if the more elaborate and complicated the system, the less room there is in it for the irrationality of human interactions. It's almost a metaphor of modern life.

My belief that the involvement with technologically related processes and active works will come to dominate artists' concerns really boils down to the fact that the possibilities are nearly unlimited. The only thing that approximates the magnitude of the possibilities is the suddenness with which they have become available. The possibilities are not just the possibilities of imagination, or of ideas applied to new materials; these have always been expressible in open-ended terms. But the possibilities of control over the physical world, of extending our personal attitudes into the active behavior of works—these are what technology gives us. And yet the technique which this statement implies is not really a technique of manual skills or factual knowledge, but a technique of understanding conceptually the many disciplines that make up technology. For me, there is a continuing problem of trying to learn about something that I wasn't taught, something that I didn't know I should know about. It means learning, simply studying all the time to find out how things work and what this knowledge may imply in another area of concern. I'm not necessarily advocating that artists or people in general do this, but I think it likely that people who already have this kind of understanding or attitude will think increasingly of themselves as artists producing work which they believe to be art, or else looking for this kind of work to regard as art. The proliferation of scientific and technical training that has come about in the last two or three decades is beginning to produce artists from its ranks, rather than through our traditional routes. I think that in time, if there is to be time, this will become the new tradition. Art is, after all, only a record of people in a time, and this is the time of technology.

The Aesthetics of
Intelligent Systems

J. W. BURNHAM

*Mr. Burnham is Associate Professor of Art at Northwestern
University and was, during the academic year 1968–1969, a
Fellow of the Center for Advanced Visual Studies at the
Massachusetts Institute of Technology. He is a sculptor and
the author of the book* Beyond Modern Sculpture.

A more accurate title for this essay would be "The Aesthetics
of Intelligent Systems—Them and Us," since the term "intelligent systems" refers not only to ourselves but also, or
more precisely, to our computer environments. Although the
art of the future could take any one of a number of directions,
it seems to me that, with the steady evolution of information-
processing techniques in our society, an increasing amount of
thought will be given to the aesthetic relationship between ourselves and our computer environments—whether or not this
relationship will eventually fall into the scope of the fine arts.

Art continues to intrigue us because it deals with ambiguous
and often obscure levels of information. Up to now, the fine-art
object has been a self-contained and finite source of information: once the art object has been created, it can only impart
its own presence. Its messages are received gradually, only
after personal revelation, and they are the delights of connois-
seurship. Yet art can also impart another kind of information,
if viewed in other contexts. More comprehensive studies and a

new historical vantage point will allow us to see art objects as they have never previously been seen.

The continued evolution of both communications and control technology bodes a new type of aesthetic relationship, very different from the one-way communication of traditional art appreciation as we know it. If, as the scientist Colin Cherry has written, "all communication proceeds by means of *signs,* with which one organism affects the behavior (or state) of another," then I suspect that the "aesthetics of intelligent systems" could be considered a dialogue where two systems gather and exchange information so as *to change constantly the states of each other.*

Pride, or the refusal to acknowledge continuity with machines, is at the bottom of man's continuing distrust of the original Industrial Revolution. This distrust is more diffuse than it was two hundred years ago, but it is still as strong. For most of the twentieth century machines have been used to make avant-garde art, but, with a few exceptions, artists have been careful to preserve the illusion of hand-made art. The decade of the nineteen-sixties dispelled that illusion. The art establishment no longer denies that machines may make art, but there is still considerable resistance to the notion that machines can be art or a direct part of the art experience. Thus, motorized art has so far been considered an aesthetic failure and has not yet secured for itself a favored niche in art history. This conclusion, however, may be premature.

Until a few years ago machines were used primarily for production and transportation. We are now entering a second age of machines, although few of its values are as yet clear either to the public or to the scientists bringing it into existence. The new machines are information-processing systems. These not only regulate production but also communicate with other machines and with human beings. The function of this technology is not the production of materials but the analysis and generation of information. It has been suggested that the field of object-production is already too well analyzed and too technically structured to provide further incentive for the artist. I tend to agree, for it now seems almost inevitable that artists will turn toward information technology as a more direct means of aesthetic activity.

To those familiar with the problems of modern art, the emphasis on the use of machines to produce a "human" form of communication will seem either reactionary or misplaced. Historically, abstract artists have rejected the work of their predecessors on the grounds of anthropomorphism, or, to put it another way, they have rejected the idealism traditionally attached to anthropomorphic imagery. Consequently, their art has reflected the contemporary tendency to maintain an "objective" or "scientific" view of reality and has managed to communicate aesthetic values only in an esoteric form.

But we must look beyond replication or illusionism to discover the basis of anthropomorphism. All art, whether abstract or representational, is in fact anthropomorphic if one considers art not in terms of appearances but in terms of its function and relation to human activity. Tools, from the simplest hand implements to the most sophisticated computers, are extensions of man's attempt to shape his environment. And in the same sense, symbols too are human extensions. According to the biologist P. D. Medawar, there are two types of evolution: endosomatic, or genetic, evolution, the slow process of hereditary change; and exosomatic, or cultural, evolution, which takes place outside the human body and applies to our tools, symbols, and other invented extensions. (The development of the space capsule is an excellent example of exosomatic evolution.) An awareness of cultural change therefore is accompanied by an understanding of anthropomorphic values rather than a rejection of them.

A cornerstone of the *l'art pour l'art* sentiment is expressed in E. M. Forster's remark: "History evolves; art stands still." For a century which has seen the resurrection of so many earlier artistic conventions, these words contain a double truth. But, in less epigrammatic terms, what Forster meant was that we cannot validly compare periods in art history as more or less advanced in development—that great art defies

Rembrandt: *Portrait of the Artist's Father,*
c. 1630. *Collection Museum of Fine Arts, Boston*

Kenneth Noland exhibition at André Emmerich
Gallery, New York, 1967

qualitative measure in degrees of sophistication or psychological effectiveness. I suspect, however, that this attitude reflects the view of Forster's generation toward art history and its particular concept of image-making and iconology, rather than revealing any innate truth about art.

For instance, let us look at two apparently disparate examples of painting: Rembrandt's portrait of his father and Kenneth Noland's work on exhibition at a gallery. The essential difference between the two is not in the paintings themselves, since both are pictorial abstractions made by covering canvas with liquid paint (it is only within the past two decades, incidentally, that we have gained enough scientific objectivity to regard Rembrandt's baroque realism as a kind of abstraction). The real difference here is in the way we are forced to look at the works of art. The Noland paintings, installed in the gallery, challenge the conventions of classical pictorial space by extending beyond the range of normal vision, beyond the limits of a frame, beyond the single viewpoint imposed on the observer of the Rembrandt portrait. We have been conditioned by art-history texts to look at art in the classical manner, as Rembrandt did, where the work is removed from its environmental context either by the frame of the painting or by the arbitrary decision of a photographer. Noland has, in this instance, restored the kind of visual communication that existed when the cave-dweller observed the red bison on the walls of the Cave of Lascaux; the distortion involved here is the result of environmental awareness rather than of the illusions of optical-iconic space. My point is McLuhanite: it is the mode of communication (the printing of the photograph of a work of art) rather than the message itself (the work of art) that has defined and leveled our response to art.

If we look at all earlier art as a form of communication— ignoring style, content, and quality—we find that the communication is a contemplative, one-way process. We have already seen in happenings, kinetic art, and luminous art some premature attempts to expand the art experience into a two-way communication loop. These art forms utilize rather crude technical means, sustaining both a real and a conceptual distance between the spectator and the work of art. As our involvement with electronic technology increases, however, the art experience may undergo a process of internalization where the constant two-way exchange of information becomes a normative goal. We should rightfully consider such a communication shift as an evolutionary step in aesthetic response.

This shift represents what could be called a figure-ground reversal in human perception of the environment. Until now, Western thought has relied upon a fixed viewer-object (or subject-stimulus) relationship, where concentration is merely a matter of shifting objectives. A great deal of technological rationalization has derived from this attitude, which has led us to think in terms of human domination and environmental passivity. The change that I perceive, however, encourages the recognition of man as an integral of his environment. The biological sciences are already beginning to realize the mistake of separating organisms from their habitat or subjects from their settings. If the computer has any experimental meaning, it will be to extend our nervous systems farther than the communications media have done so far.

We tend to think of the computer at its present stage of development as a super-fast calculator or data file; few of us conceive of it as a system which can reorganize many remote environments and channel them into a sustained and coherent experience. One of the truisms of innovation is that all inventions begin by taking the shape of the device which they have superseded. For instance, one computer scientist told me that many present computer applications are analogous to trying to fit a steam engine to the body of an iron horse. Like many of us, most artists still envision the computer as an iron horse. Their approaches usually stem from a desire to see the computer as an elegant tool for making traditional art. Since the early and middle nineteen-sixties, scientists such as Michael Noll and Kenneth Knowlton of Bell Laboratories in New Jersey have pioneered in the development of computer graphics. As a rule, their attempts to use printout devices have produced art which is very similar to examples of modern painting. I must point out, however, that the original purpose of most of this work has been scientific rather than artistic experimentation.

Taking a different approach, the sculptor Johan Severtson uses the computer to program parameters for his sculptures. The resulting data give him literally hundreds of possible compositional variations from which to choose. Utilizing the best patterns, he fabricates large plate-aluminum sculptures. At one point I suggested to Severtson that his pages of computer data, which can be seen as drawings of exquisite variation, were more intriguing than the resulting sculpture. Interestingly, for the past two years Severtson has concentrated upon filming the computer in the process of designing, and he has shown the films as integral parts of the works of art.

One of the most obvious uses of the computer is to create anthropomorphized sculptures. With a Dada sense of humor, Ed Kienholz created *The Friendly Gray Computer—Star Gauge Model 54.* Essentially, it is a chassis set on rockers, with a few active lights and motors forming the semblance of a face. Kienholz seems to be saying that after all computers feel too, but he also makes it clear that we are confronted with an unknown and potentially dangerous species.

Another pioneer in the use of cybernetic principles and, recently, of computers is the French-Hungarian artist Nicolas Schöffer. In 1956 the artist previewed his first responsive sculpture, *CYSP 1,* at the Sarah Bernhardt Theater in Paris. This early venture, a tall skeletal structure with spinning disks and beacons which responds to light and sound, let to Schöffer's *Cybernetic Light Tower,* a structure over a thousand feet high which monitors and reports on various conditions in the Paris environment. His efforts do not reflect the values of a cybernated city however, but the values of an artist trying to automate a monumental sculpture. Schöffer's work has a kind of nineteen-twenties and -thirties futurism about it—strikingly like the stills from Alexander Korda's motion picture *Worlds to Come.*

These examples of computer-oriented art are mentioned because they represent some of the better-known attempts to date. By formalist art standards, or in terms of everyday interest, they are not terribly exciting, but as experiments they force us to think about the implications of a very important new tool. During the summer of 1968 the Institute of Contemporary Art in London presented "Cybernetic Serendipity," an exhibition of cybernetic and computer-oriented art from all over the world. The show contained a few of the works I have mentioned, as well as exhibits illustrating the history of cybernetics; some results of various attempts to use the computer in the creation of poetry, music, dance, films, and architecture; and a number of cybernetic artifacts designed by scientists and engineers.

During a conversation I had with Miss Jasia Reichardt, the curator of "Cybernetic Serendipity," she lamented the fact that so few artists are concerned with the use of computers. She felt that the ideas of scientists dealing with the creative implications of computers were considerably more interesting than what artists had to say about the uses of information-processing technology. Miss Reichardt deplored above all the dearth of computer-supported exhibits which could be shown in museums; time, money, and technical complications have put the majority of them out of reach. "Where *is* all the computer art?" summed up her feelings.

Significantly, Europe has been the breeding ground for a school of scientists, artists, and philosophers involved with the aesthetic implications of computer theory. *Kunst und Kybernetik,* a book published in 1968 in West Germany, contained a number of papers on the subject, and in the summer of 1968 several contributors to the book gathered for an international symposium on "Computers and Visual Research" during the exhibition "New Tendencies No. 4" in Zagreb. Much of the discussion centered on the information-theory analysis of traditional and computer graphic art. Yet the amount of art or art study done with the aid of a computer in Europe is small, except possibly in West Germany, where a relatively large number of computers is in operation. More important than the number of computers, however, is the availability of free computer time. Countries without computer time for nonessential tasks can devote nothing to art, although the desire to do such research may be there. It is ironic that in the United States, where there is a surplus of computer time, no concerted attempt has been made to use the computer as an art tool. Perhaps this is no more than an indication of our priorities.

Although "Cybernetic Serendipity" had significance as a historical event—the first comprehensive exhibition of computer-derived art—its real meaning lay in those doubts and disappointments expressed by Jasia Reichardt. We are dealing with an art mode whose aesthetic dimensions have not yet been fully comprehended by the artist. McLuhan reflected that IBM did not skyrocket in growth until it decided that its task was information-processing rather than the business of selling office machines. Indeed, a computer-systems specialist once told me that his hardest job was to convince corporations that it was dangerously shortsighted to follow five-year plans. These observations tell us something about the essential nature of the computer. Used to its fullest, the computer is a part of a continual system and, as such, it processes information metabolically. In other words, the computer is not a problem-solver in the classic sense, but a means by which information is directed incrementally toward the maintenance of a constant level of stability, a function similar to that of the human nervous system.

The computer's most profound aesthetic implication is that we are being forced to dismiss the classical view of art and reality which insists that man stand outside of reality in order to observe it, and, in art, requires the presence of the picture frame and the sculpture pedestal. The notion that art can be separated from its everyday environment is a cultural fixation, as is the ideal of objectivity in science. It may be that the computer will negate the need for such an illusion by fusing both observer and observed, "inside" and "outside." It has already been observed that the everyday world is rapidly assuming identity with the condition of art.

Exhibition of works by Niki de St. Phalle and Jean Tinguely in
Central Park, summer 1968 *(Photo courtesy New York City
Parks Department)*

Dennis Oppenheim: *Pennsylvania Wheat Piece*, 1968

My last point can be illustrated by viewing the contrast in the two environments pictured. The first is an outdoor exhibition held in Central Park in 1967 of machine sculptures and *Nanas* by Jean Tinguely and Niki de St. Phalle. As you can see, a hedge-covered fence and various signs clearly indicate to every pedestrian that the art is not to be touched. In a sense, the hedge and padlocked gate surrounding the garden serve the same purpose as the frame around an oil painting: they tell the onlooker that the sculptured animals are to be experienced but that they do not exist in the "real" environment where casual involvement is possible. On the other hand, Dennis Oppenheim's *200' × 900' Wheat Field*, which was executed on a farm in Pennsylvania during the same summer, is an example of art without boundaries. Here the artist directed the mowing, baling, gathering, and unloading of a portion of the crop, considering each activity as a part of his art. Only the fact that the artist himself has selected the site and the direction of the work separates his activity from that of the farmer's. Such an endeavor is very close to what is called conceptual art.

In *Duration Piece* #9 Douglas Huebler conceived of a series of space-time transactions as a "site sculpture." The mailing of a box to six locations across the country and the return of registered-mail receipts defined a straightline trajectory of the art work across the United States. What intrigues me is not the resulting documents but the fact that a work of art using a public communication channel was conceived and executed. Artistic volition is the only factor which separates it from millions of similar acts. This ordinariness implies no lack of artistry, but rather the realization that art does not have to be physically isolated or tangible to be effective.

The word "environment" has recently been used to define a popular alternative to painting and sculpture, the traditional modes of art-making. Many environments are paintings or sculptures, or a combination, structured to fill a room-sized space. If we consider this accepted form of art environment in terms of our previous discussion of a computer environment, we come to some interesting conclusions. First, most art en-

Douglas Huebler: Documentation for *Duration Piece #9*,
January–February 1969. 10,045 miles. Time: 64 days.
Berkeley, Calif.; Riverton, Ut.; Ellsworth, Neb.; Alpha, Ia.;
Tuscola, Mich.; Hull, Mass.

vironments are pre-eminently contrived. Second, if computer
environments are just now becoming the means by which we
extend our senses in order to increase our knowledge of an environment and, perhaps, to establish a dialogue with elements
within that environment, then we should not expect too much
as yet from artists.

Nevertheless, various artists have tried to produce situations
where the spectator's presence has triggered bits of information. For example, Anthony Martin recently produced a *Game
Room* (1968), a series of floor spaces which, if stood upon,
would bombard one with "mixed media." At the same time,
Jean Dupuy and Ralph Martel constructed *Heart Beats Dust*,
which consists of a palpitating pile of lithol rubine, a very fine,
brilliant red pigment. A 15-inch speaker mounted under a rub-
ber membrane vibrates the lithol rubine, which produces wave

Pulsa: *Light-and-Sound Installation*, January–March 1969.
Yale Golf Course, New Haven, Conn.

patterns. In a version shown at the Brooklyn Museum's "Some More Beginnings" exhibition, spectators could vibrate the speaker by holding a microphone next to their hearts. I should also mention James Seawright's *Electronic Peristyle* (1968), a circular array of twelve black formica columns containing lights, blowers, and sound-generating equipment.[1] Here the interruption of photoelectric circuits by the spectator produces a series of sounds, light patterns, and breezes. While some margin of ambiguity as to the meaning of the stimuli and their relation to the spectator is permissible and even desirable in such a work, Seawright's *Electronic Peristyle* fails to build into a coherent or aesthetically meaningful experience, and this remains a central deficiency of most art predicated upon the feedback principle.

Other problems arise in the Pulsa Group's computer-driven, strobe-light outdoor installations. Centered around the New Haven and Boston areas, these are the most ambitious programed art environments to date. Pulsa has used components of analogue and digital computers to produce high-speed con-

[1] See illustration earlier in this book, in James Seawright's "Phenomenal Art: Form, Idea, and Technique."—ED.

figurations in sound and light. These patterns are permuta-
tional, hence almost infinite in variety. Spread out over several
acres of rolling lawns, the Pulsa environments physically transcend the quasi-painting results of other programed-light art
forms produced to date. The experience of walking through a
Pulsa installation is essentially that of encountering random
strobe-light bursts. Patterns appear only when one is to some
degree removed from the field of lights. As a group, Pulsa is not
insensitive to the need for using a computer more elegantly. Its
members talk of the computer as an environmental sensing device for structuring human participation in the environment.
The lack of adequate financial backing is a major obstacle to
their plans.

It would seem that all responsive environments, whether
computerized or natural, have the same prerequisite—that is,
some semblance of intelligence. We speak of intelligent organisms, but we must acknowledge that environments possess a
level of intelligence too, depending upon the richness of ecological channels of communication. Some ecologists feel that we
can rightly speak only of a symbiotic intelligence, that of the
organism-environment. In a similar way, many humanists and
naturalists lament the loss of man's prescientific sensitivity
to changes and conditions in the natural environment. They regard technology as an instrument for dulling receptiveness, and
consider that technology, at best, has given us a false sense of
security. Obviously there is substantial truth to these asser-
tions. A technological environment monitors only the things
that seem most essential to it. This fact may account in part
for the tragic decay of our natural surroundings. But I suspect
that this decay is primarily due to behavioral patterns of the
mechanical age, and I believe that the computer can help to
transcend this condition. Used with more wisdom than we appear to have now, computer systems can sensitize us to information in the environment that would otherwise be ignored.

Another simple responsive environment is Hans Haacke's
Photo-Electric Viewer-Programed Coordinate System. Haacke's
room contains a grid of infrared light beams and photo-

Hans Haacke: *Photo-Electric Viewer-Programed Coordinate System,* 1966–1968

resistor switches which are nearly invisible to the spectator. The switches control the lights just above them, so that the spectator defines his own presence by reading the light grid. Haacke would like to eliminate specific light sources like the row of light bulbs used and to utilize only the pale and diffused illumination from the wall itself. The spectator's relationship with the room and his ensuing aesthetic experience are precipitated by his own bodily activities; no contemplation of or empathizing with an object is necessary.

Les Levine considers television to be an environmental tool because it is integrated into our lives to the point where it is invisible. Levine's first major television piece was *Iris,* a battery of television monitors and cameras that scanned their immediate vicinity. Although *Iris* appears as an iconic presence, the artist has rejected the painter's use of television as an abstract pattern-generator, considering it a trivial function. Levine demonstrated the kind of responsive environment that television can be in his use of three monitors and cameras during a panel discussion at New York University's Loeb Center. The artist was asked to appear with several other speakers,

Les Levine: *Television Piece*, 1968. *Loeb Student Center,
New York University*

but chose instead to show himself as a group of television
images. Like the computer, television becomes an environment
embedded within the more pervasive physical environment
which we associate with day-to-day reality.

At this point I want to shift my discussion from the efforts
of artists who deal with electronic information-processing to
those of scientists. If "intelligent systems" can refer to computer environments, then we are dealing with a dichotomy of
human and nonbiological intelligence. Let me briefly compare
the brain and the computer as information-processing systems.
The human brain has an excellent capacity for retrieving and
juxtaposing stored information. Its number of intercon-
nections is very high, running into the billions. As a general-
purpose problem-solver, it far transcends any machine made to
date. Computers, on the other hand, can handle tremendous
amounts of information for extended periods of time, but operate in much more routine ways than the brain does. Unlike the
brain, most computers are incapable either of organizing themselves or of comparing disparate types of information. As one
scientist put it, computers are like very quick but stupid chil-

dren who must be told everything in explicit detail. Intelligence can be generally defined as the ability to solve a wide variety of problems in many environments. If that is accurate and not merely anthropomorphic, then it is clear why human beings still outthink computers in most circumstances.

The possibilities of nonbiological intelligence were first explored in the writings of Allen Turing, John von Neumann, and Ross Ashby, three pioneers of cybernetics and computer theory. During the early days of computer development (1950–1959) there were extravagant hopes and speculations for solving the riddle of human intelligence by duplicating it. Repeated failures have elicited extreme caution and, in some cases, downright pessimism in the scientific world.

Let us examine briefly some of the most important approaches so far to the problem of producing nonbiological intelligence, an area where the concepts of intelligent environment and computer environment begin to merge. Although the computer environment is still severely limited by the computer's inflexibility and by its extremely narrow range of contact with the outside world, and although the problem of simulating human intelligence is far from solved, enormous advances have been made in computer technology over the past fifteen years to the point where the computer[2] has become a prime factor in the analysis of any social philosophy of the future. Although there are basic differences between an art environment, where all information is given in the form of applied physical-visual effects, and a computer environment, which is concerned with the amplification and exchange of information, I believe it is not unreasonable to envision a future of art in terms of these significant developments.

"Artificial intelligence" is a term frequently used to denote the use of heuristic and algorithmic computer programs in various areas of problem-solving, such as pattern-recognition, search methods, learning processes, and language-translation. Some critics have insisted that such programs can never equal

[2] Note that I have used the word "computer" in a general sense, since computers today are actually computer systems comprising many types of machines.

human intelligence, since they are based on a partial understanding of only some of the techniques employed by the brain.
And the fact remains that computer systems lack the sensory
equipment necessary to deal adequately with the outside world.
As Seymour Papert, one expert in the field, has pointed out, we
deprive the machine of the means of experiencing reality as we
do and "then complain that machines cannot be intelligent.
We're like people who put pigs in filthy sties and call them
dirty animals."

The Architecture Machine was developed at Massachusetts
Institute of Technology by the architect Nicolas Negroponte
and Marvin Minsky, one of the pioneers of artificial-intelligence
research. This is a computer system in which a problem-solving
capacity has been linked with sensing devices in order to discover and reorganize an environment. A computer-linked camera monitors a pile of white blocks on a flat black background,
and the resulting monocular picture of the pile describes meas-
urements, perspective, sides, joints, and texture, in that order

Nicolas Negroponte and Marvin Minsky: The Architecture Machine,
1968. *Massachusetts Institute of Technology*

of importance, so that the computer may instruct a hydraulic arm to fit new blocks into place. The addition of cameras would give the computer a clear three-dimensional picture of the blocks so that the arm could add or subtract blocks to make up new spatial configurations. This is an instance, such as Papert mentioned, where the computer input and output devices are "trained," like a small child, to see the world, rather than being given a picture of the world as a predigested program. Negroponte envisions the Architecture Machine ultimately as a centrally located data bank connected to the building patterns, utilities, and demographic problems of a city. In effect, it could become a metabolic planner, dealing with a city's problems in "real time"—that is, as problems arise.

As a professor of electrical engineering at MIT, Marvin Minsky has been one of the chief defenders and critics of artificial-intelligence research. While his chess programs and ball-catching robots have received much publicity, less is generally known about his brilliant analysis of finite machines and its effect in demolishing many of the illusions surrounding experiments in artificial intelligence. In talking with Minsky one finds that he is a rationalist, the likes of which make the French Encyclopedists appear church faithful. He is convinced that free will and intelligence are culturally sustained myths— like the traditional concept of art. Minsky does concede that art is stimulating because it brings out some of the more noble and sensitive characteristics of man, but he insists that art remains intellectually underdeveloped precisely because the fundamental questions of art, of its existence and purpose, remain undefined. (I was tempted to add that the same is true of mathematics.)

As a scientist with some ability for composing and performing music, Minsky maintains that the intellectual competence of a great artist such as Beethoven is considerably below the reasoning powers of any major scientist, a view that most cultural anthropologists and clinical psychologists would have trouble supporting. Out of this conflict arises one of the dangers cited by moral critics of machine thinking: if such activity

Automaton Vehicle, 1963-1968. Stanford
Research Institute

becomes a reality, the scientist is liable to bias it by his own
specialized view of intelligent behavior.

At Stanford Research Institute in Menlo Park, California,
scientist Charles Rosen and his staff have developed an Automaton Vehicle. This device is connected by radio to a time-
sharing computer. Its camera and logic-control unit work with
four sensory systems: tactile sensors, an optical range finder, a
shape-describing television camera, and a navigation system.
The Automaton Vehicle moves about the room, touching the
geometric objects shown in the photograph. From these experiences it builds an internal map—rather like a person becoming accustomed to a room in the dark. Although the ro-
bot's sensing devices are varied and highly sophisticated, the
process of interpreting and using sensory data remains com-

paratively primitive. Yet many different excursions around the room can succeed in giving the vehicle a usable "past."

Bionics and research in self-organizing systems are two closely related alternatives to developing artificial intelligence. Both attempt to simulate or reproduce aspects of living organisms, such as self-organization, which seems to be a property unique in intelligent life, involving perception, growth, learning, development of neural structure, and the effects of environmental feedback. Practical goals of this research include supplementing human sensory capacities and improving human intelligence through genetic engineering.

The implications of bionic research were brought out by an editorial in the *IEEE Spectrum* magazine (August 1967) entitled "Man, a Subsystem?" It emphasized that nothing more than anthropomorphic vanity accounted for sending men into space on jobs that machines could be made to accomplish more efficiently, pointing out: "As a subsystem, man leaves much to be desired. What other system has no significant prospect of miniaturization or ruggedization, can work at full capacity only one quarter of the time, must be treated as non-expendable, requires a critical psychological and physical environment, cannot be decontaminated, and is so unpredictable?"

All efforts to produce nonbiological intelligence depend upon an organism-environment relationship. As previously mentioned, this may be humanly interpreted as a "program" or, as in the case of the MIT and Stanford robots, the environment may be a limited portion of the real world. Another approach is described as "evolutionary programing," in which the "organism" and "environment" are numerically simulated through two linked computer systems. The "environment" is a generated number series. Survival depends upon the organism's logically predicting the number series. The organism, or the computer's problem-solving strategy, is randomly altered and the new organism must predict the environment or it is discarded for the original strategy. In this way the next generation is always heir to a successful strategy, and thus organism and environment evolve together. "Quick-time" computer operations allow many mutations and generations of problem-solving to evolve in a matter of minutes. Such an approach has significance for the other areas of study in nonbiological intelligence, for, as Marvin Minsky has said, "Once we have developed a firm evolutionary technique, the development of artifical intelligence will come quickly."

For art, possibly the most significant form of nonbiological intelligence, or hyperbiological intelligence, is that of "human enhancement through man-machine relationships." Briefly, this includes all efforts to learn and solve problems through interactive, time-sharing computer programs, where a person communicates directly with the program through one or more terminal devices. The objective is to think creatively with the computer in "real time," or in the time it takes to carry on a normal conversation. Joseph Licklider, director of Project MAC at MIT (Machine-Assisted Cognition is one of several names for this project), believes that such time-sharing systems will have immense impact upon our culture—in all phases of life, including art—during the nineteen-seventies. When I pressed him to verify this statement, he responded with two other statistics.

Licklider believes in the dynamics of exponential growth. The population, he states, doubles every thirty years; the amount of information doubles every fifteen years; and the number of computers and other types of information-processing equipment doubles every two years. He also asserts that within ten to twenty years computers will engage in activities and show a high intelligence that no one can dispute. In 1967 at the Metropolitan Museum of Art in a seminar on the use of computers in museums, Licklider suggested that some of the restraints have to be removed from computers as communication devices before they become acceptable tools to the artist. He sees the need for larger, brighter, and more interactive display tubes, and also for terminal equipment sensitive to light patterns, vibrations, pressure, textures, and sounds—in other words, the full array of sensory input-output devices available in human communication.

While these are ideal goals, Licklider also touched upon more practical considerations for the aesthetic use of interactive systems, such as the technological lag, where cost, general usability, and proliferation of means will determine when and how the artist can use computers for direct creativity. He believes that there will be an evolution in the artist's use of applied technology. Up to now the artist has been involved in building relatively simple machines that turn lights on and off or move components. Because of advances in computer technology, however, artists will probably be forced to concentrate on programing existing equipment rather than building more hardware. Licklider points out that we are gradually "turning up the gain" (amplifying the message) in all areas of communication, education, entertainment, and art. The computer is potentially the best available means for reinforcing these communication loops with the human brain, because if something is not interactive, it is nonmotivating. However, he insists, one should expect considerable resistance to any shift of art in this direction. For one thing, intellectuals need less interaction than most people; this fact accounts for their strength and weakness. Consequently, intellectuals have a large capacity for sustained involvement with one-way symbolic systems, and painting and sculpture are among the more treasured of these symbologies.

During the past year I was invited, as an artist, to learn to use the time-sharing computer system at MIT's Lincoln Laboratories. I was fortunate to have for teachers two men deeply interested in making the computer a creative tool and in allowing artists access to a computer: Oliver Selfridge, a mathematician by training and one of the pioneers in artificial-intelligence research; and Jack Nolan, currently president of the Massachusetts College of Art and formerly Group Systems Leader at Lincoln Laboratories. They are both dedicated to the goal of enabling the untrained layman to use a computer almost immediately and they believe that the entire field of artificial-intelligence research is highly overrated and misguided. Selfridge feels that the future lies with a man-computer symbiosis, and that "so far the creative person in the computer environment is highly frustrated. Computers are not yet flexible enough. The answer is to reward lazy people who demand easier and more understandable computer languages by giving them these languages."

I studied the rudiments of one language, FORTRAN, using a primer written by Oliver Selfridge. Its goal is to teach conversation with a time-sharing computer in very much the same way a child learns to speak: by trying different word combinations and waiting for a desired response. Using this, I never studied the structure of the computer's system, or the grammar of FORTRAN, but only attempted to communicate with the computer and to become familiar with the "computer environment" as if I were adjusting my thinking to the intellectual capabilities of a new acquaintance in conversation.

I then began to learn a computer display language, CAFE, which was developed by Jack Nolan for making constructions

Jack Burnham at console, Computer Room, Massachusetts Institute of Technology, Lincoln Laboratory, Lexington, Mass., 1968

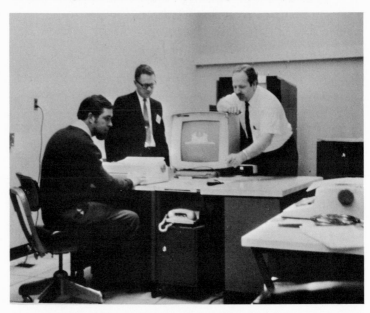

using only straight-line segments. This is a simplified language which develops some types of figures rather slowly, but which is still considerably faster than feeding the computer punch-card instructions. Using a special camera attached to a CRT screen, I found this is an excellent and relatively inexpensive way to create animated movies in a few hours or a few days. Eventually, however, the lack of content and dynamic variety in the program may prove to be a drawback for the artist. The illustration shows two computer specialists and myself seated in front of an IBM 2250 display unit. This is attached to an IBM 360, Model 67, time-sharing computer.

Selfridge and Nolan took for granted that, once mastered, the computer would be a superb artistic tool for generating graphic designs. Perhaps it is, but as an artist I found the real challenge of a computer to be in discovering a program's memory, interactive ability, and logic functions. One gradually learns to conceptualize an entirely abstract model of the program. As with one's own mind, parts are brought out for inspection as needed. Moreover, a dialogue *evolves* between the participants—the computer program and the human subject—so that both move beyond their original state. Of course it is unrealistic to expect artists to begin to use computers the way they use paints, canvas, and welded steel. As a rule, new and exotic technology has not led to the production of great or even good art. Somehow the aesthetic implications of a technology become manifest only when it becomes pervasively, if not subconsciously, present in the life-style of a culture. In terms of a public utility, we are at least ten to fifteen years away from the kinds of machine creativity that I have discussed. But if I have tried to make an argument for an eventual evolution toward two-way communication in art, it is because present social circumstances point in that direction.

In spite of much dissatisfaction with the results of technology in this century, I cannot believe that the world would willingly revert to a less sophisticated technological level; that could happen only by accident. We now witness all the signs of environmental decay: urban systems breakdown, greater crime,

pollution, resource depletion, and political rebellion. Because
socially structured self-interest has effectively prevented us
from dealing with these interconnected problems, some social
scientists feel that the process of group decision-making is on
the verge of collapse in many of the large industrialized
countries. The current dissension may be the result of a basic
fault in communication—if we assume that it is education that
encourages enlightened self-interest. In the next decade two-
way public television, household computer systems linked to
data banks, and voting by telephone will become technically
feasible. Is there any reason, however, to believe that these
systems will be used with any more wisdom than public television is now?

My conjecture is that computers will radically reorganize
social values, although in the first stages they may do it badly.
I believe that they will be seen as one of the few reasonable alternatives to continued social, technical, and ecological chaos.
My hope is that the initial complexity of these information
systems will not prevent substantial numbers of artists from
using and thinking about them. Insensitive and indiscriminate
handling of information in central data banks will become a
major and political. issue, as will the progressive withdrawal
of human creativity from semiautomated industries. One begins to hear about a "sanitized elite," answerable to nobody,
who will control all information going into their own data files.
Wealth and ownership might cease to be the prerequisites of
power as access to and control of information take their place.
My conversations with computer scientists impel me to believe
that these are not idle fears. Practiced in a free environment,
art is political in that it reveals cultural inhibitions and symptoms of repression. Even if art is a form of metacommunication
and only indirectly political, it has much to lose by not involving itself with these extremely subtle and potent media.

Involvements with such information-processing techniques
as I have described are bound to provoke structural shifts in the
art world. Here are a few as I see them. The traditional notion
of consecrated art objects and settings will gradually give way

to the conclusion that art is *conceptual focus,* and that the boundary conditions of form as process and system transcend the more literal notions of geometrically defined form. Thus any space-time fragment of reality may serve as subject matter. The breakdown and confusion between canonical art forms will continue until it is agreed that they place a false emphasis on physical and sensual isolation as prerequisites for aesthetic valuation.

As the computer environment further condenses the known world and as it increasingly becomes an elegant surrogate for global experience, a profound change will take place in the acquisition of knowledge and sensitivity. Until very recently the machine-age Protestant ethic placed a high value on learned knowledge, since one-way learning through print demands great patience and repetitious labor. And as John McHale has pointed out, our "cultivated aesthetic taste is also associated with the acquisition of hard-won understanding." As we begin to treat art environments as pure "lived experience," we realize the strong parallel between the symbology of the printed page and the structural and iconographic complexities of "appreciating" a painting or sculpture. The processing of electronic informa-tion between two systems is pre-eminently lived experience, and thus learning-feeling-sensing appear to be effortless. Al-ready critics oriented to the literate-optical tradition have ex-pressed profound distrust of art environments "where there is nothing to be seen or interpreted."

The secularization of art will continue. I suspect that there will be a gradual phasing out of artists and art training in the conventional sense. One computer specialist said to me, "You think machines are only capable of sterile, mechanically perfect products? Give us the time and demand and we will show you better 'handcrafted' goods than any person can make." It will be interesting to see if we phase out all handcrafts as economic liabilities or maintain them under some ideological pretext of their importance to human existence. It seems reasonable to predict that artists may function in a wide range of occupa-tions, no longer identified with a few medieval crafts, and will be recognized as people who, within the limits of their fields, solve problems in unique and particularly elegant ways.

Gradually we may realize that the conditions of art are contingent upon our understanding of human communication. From what I have suggested here, it may seem that the electronic technologies are making deep inroads into this most private of all mysteries. But if we are to believe the great linguist Noam Chomsky, we know next to nothing about language and and intercommunication. As long as this holds true, the survival of art is assured.

Art as a Form
of Reality

HERBERT MARCUSE

Professor Marcuse, born and educated in Germany, has lived in the United States since 1934. He has taught philosophy and politics at Columbia University, Harvard, and Brandeis, and is now at the University of California, San Diego. He is the author of several important books, including One-Dimensional Man *and* Eros and Civilization.

The thesis of the end of Art has become a familiar slogan: radicals of the New Left take it as a truism; they reject or "suspend" Art as part of bourgeois culture, just as they reject or suspend its literature, its philosophy. This verdict extends easily to all theory, all intelligence (no matter how "creative") that does not spark action, practice, that does not noticeably help to change the world, that does not—be it only for a short time—break through this universe of mental and physical pollution in which we live. Music does it, with song and dance: the music which activates the body; the songs which no longer sing but cry and shout. (To measure the road traveled in the last thirty years, compare the "traditional," classical tone and text of the songs of the Spanish Civil War with today's songs of protest and defiance. Or compare the "classical" theater of Brecht with the Living Theater of today.)

We witness not only the political but also, and primarily, the

artistic attack on Art in all its forms, on Art as Form[1] itself.
The distance and dissociation of Art from reality are denied,
refused, and destroyed; if Art is still anything at all, it must be
real, part and parcel of life—but of a life which is itself the
conscious negation of the established way of life, with all its
institutions, with its entire material and intellectual culture,
its entire immoral morality, its required and its clandestine
behavior, its work and its fun.

A double reality has emerged (or re-emerged), that of those
who say "no" and that of those who say "yes." Those engaged in whatever artistic effort is still "valid" refuse to say
"yes" both to reality and to Art. Yet the refusal itself *is* also
reality: very real are the young who have no more patience, who
have, with their own bodies and minds, experienced the horrors
and the oppressive comforts of the given reality; real are the
ghettos and their spokesmen; real are the forces of liberation
all over the globe, East and West, First, Second, and Third
World. But the meaning of this reality to those who experience
it can no longer be communicated in the established language
and images—in the available forms of expression, no matter
how new, how radical they may be.

What is at stake is the vision, the experience of a reality that
is so fundamentally different, so antagonistic to the prevailing
reality that any communication through the established means
seems to reduce this difference, to vitiate this experience. And
this irreconcilability with the very medium of communication
also extends to the forms of Art themselves, to Art as Form.
From the position of today's rebellion and refusal, Art itself
appears as part and force of the tradition which perpetuates
that which *is* and prevents the realization of that which can
and ought to be. And Art does so precisely inasmuch as it *is*
Form, because the artistic Form (no matter how *anti*-Art it
strives to be) arrests that which is in motion, gives it limit and
frame and place in the prevailing universe of experience and

---

[1] I shall use the term *Art* (capitalized) as including not only the visual arts
but also literature and music. I shall use the term *Form* (capitalized) as that
which defines Art as Art, that is to say, as essentially (ontologically) different not only from (everyday) reality but also from such other manifestations
of intellectual culture as science and philosophy.

aspirations, gives it a value *in* this universe, makes it an object among others. And this means that, in this universe, the work of art, as well as of antiart, becomes *exchange* value, commodity. And it is precisely the Commodity Form, as the form of reality, which is the target of today's rebellion.

True, the commercialization of Art is not new, and not even of very recent date. It is as old as bourgeois society. The process gains momentum with the almost unlimited reproducibility of the work of art, by virtue of which the *œuvre* becomes susceptible to imitation and repetition even in its finest and most sublime achievements. In his masterful analysis of this process, Walter Benjamin has shown that there is one thing which militates against all reproduction, namely, the "aura" of the *œuvre*, the unique historical situation in which the work of art is created, into which it speaks and which defines its function and meaning. As soon as the *œuvre* leaves its own historical moment, which is unrepeatable and unredeemable, its "original" truth is falsified, or (more cautiously) modified: it acquires a different meaning, responding (affirmatively or negatively) to the different historical situation. Owing to new instruments and techniques, to new forms of perception and thought, the original *œuvre* may now be interpreted, instrumented, "translated," and thus become richer, more complex, refined, fuller of meaning. Nevertheless, the fact remains that it is no longer what it *was* to the artist and his audience and public.

And yet, through all these changes, something remains identically the same: the *œuvre* itself, to which all these modifications happen. The most "updated" work of art is still the particular, unique work of art, updated. What kind of entity *is* it which remains the identical "substance" of all its modifications?

It is not the "plot": Sophocles' tragedy shares the "story" of Oedipus with many other literary expressions; it is not the "object" of a painting, which recurs innumerable times (as general category: portrait of a man sitting, standing; mountainous landscape, et cetera); it is not the stuff, the raw material of which the work is made. What constitutes the unique and enduring identity of an *œuvre,* and what makes a *work* into a work of *art*—this entity is the Form. By virtue of the Form, and the Form alone, the content achieves that uniqueness which makes it the content of one particular work of art and of no other. The way in which the story is told; the structure and selectiveness of verse and prose; that which is *not* said, *not* represented, and yet is present; the interrelations of lines and colors and points—these are some aspects of the Form which remove, dissociate, alienate the *œuvre* from the given reality and make it enter into its own reality: the realm of forms.

The realm of forms: it is a *historical* reality, an irreversible sequence of styles, subjects, techniques, rules—each inseparably related to its society and repeatable only as imitation. However, in all their almost infinite diversity they are but variations of the one Form which distinguishes Art from any other product of human activity. Ever since Art left the magical stage, ever since it ceased to be "practical," to be one "technique" among others—that is to say, ever since it became a separate branch of the social division of labor—it assumed a Form of its own, common to all arts.

This Form corresponded to the new function of Art in society: to provide the "holiday," the elevation, the break in the terrible routine of life—to present something "higher," "deeper," perhaps "truer" and better, satisfying needs not satisfied in daily work and fun, and therefore pleasurable. (I am speaking of the social, the "objective" historical function of Art; I am not speaking of what Art is to the artist, not of his intentions and goals, which are of a very different order.) In other, more brutal words: Art is not (or is not supposed to be) a use-value to be consumed in the course of the daily performances of men; its utility is of a transcendent kind, utility for the soul or the mind which does not enter the normal behavior of men and does not really change it—except for just that short period of elevation, the cultured holiday: in church, in the museum, in the concert hall, in the theater, before the monuments and ruins of the great past. And after the break, real life continues: business as usual.

With these features, Art becomes a force *in* the (given) society, but not *of* the (given) society. Produced in and for the established reality, providing it with the beautiful and the sublime, elevation and pleasure, Art also dissociates itself from this reality and confronts it with another one: the beautiful and the sublime, the pleasure and the truth that Art presents are not merely those obtaining in the actual society. No matter how much Art may be determined, shaped, directed by prevailing values, standards of taste and behavior, limits of experience, et cetera, it is always more and other than beautification and sublimation, recreation and validation of that which is. Even the most realistic *œuvre* constructs a reality of its own: its men and women, its objects, its landscape, its music reveal what remains unsaid, unseen, unheard in everyday life. Art is "alienating."

As part of the *established* culture, Art is *affirmative,* sustaining this culture; as *alienation* from the established reality, Art is a *negating* force. The *history of Art* can be understood as the *harmonization of this antagonism.*

The material, stuff, and data of Art (words, sounds, lines, and colors; but also thoughts, emotions, images) are ordered, interrelated, defined, and "contained" in the *œuvre* in such a manner that they constitute a structured whole—closed, in its external appearance, between the two covers of a book, in a frame, at a specific place; its presentation takes a specific time, before and after which is the *other* reality, daily life. In its effect on the recipient, the *œuvre* itself may endure and recur; but it will remain, as recurrent, a self-contained whole, a mental or sensuous object clearly separated and distinct from (real) things. The laws or rules governing the organization of the elements in the *œuvre* as a unified whole seem of infinite variety, but the classical aesthetic tradition has given them a common denominator: they are supposed to be guided by the idea of the *beautiful.*

This central idea of classical aesthetics invokes the sensibility as well as the rationality of man, pleasure principle and reality principle: the work of art is to appeal to the senses, to satisfy sensuous needs—but in a highly sublimated manner. Art is to have a reconciling, a tranquilizing, *and* a cognitive function, to be beautiful *and* true. The beautiful was to lead to the truth: *in* the beautiful, a truth was supposed to appear that did not, and could not, appear in any other form.

Harmonization of the beautiful and the true—what was supposed to make up the essential unity of the work of art— has turned out to be an increasingly impossible *unification of opposites,* for the true has appeared as increasingly incompatible with the beautiful. Life, the human condition, has militated increasingly against the sublimation of reality in the Form of Art.

This sublimation is not primarily (and perhaps not at all!) a process in the psyche of the artist but rather an ontological condition, pertaining to the *Form* of Art itself. It necessitates an organization of the material into the unity and enduring stability of the *œuvre,* and this organization "succumbs," as it were, to the idea of the beautiful. It is as if this idea would impose itself upon the material through the creative energy of the artist (though by no means as his conscious intention). The result is most evident in those works which are the uncompromisingly "direct" accusation of reality. The artist indicts—but the indictment anesthetizes the terror. Thus, the brutality, stupidity, horror of war are all there in the work of Goya, but as "pictures" they are caught up in the dynamic of aesthetic transfiguration—they can be admired, side by side with the glorious portraits of the king who presided over the horror. The Form contradicts the content and triumphs over the content—at the price of its anesthetization. The immediate, unsublimated (physiological and psychological) response, vomiting, crying fury, gives way to the aesthetic experience: germane response to the work of Art.

The character of this aesthetic sublimation, essential to Art and inseparable from its history as part of affirmative culture, has found its perhaps most striking formulation in Kant's concept of *interesseloses Wohlgefallen*: delight, pleasure divorced from all interest, desire, inclination. The aesthetic object is, as it were, without a particular subject, or rather without any relation to a subject other than that of pure contemplation—pure eye, pure ear, pure mind. Only in this purification of ordinary experience and its objects, only in this transfiguration of reality do the aesthetic universe and the aesthetic object emerge as pleasurable, beautiful, and sublime. In other, and more brutal, words: the precondition for Art is a radical looking into reality and a looking away from it—a repression of its immediacy, and of the immediate response to it. It is the *œuvre* itself which *is*, and which achieves this repression; and as aesthetic repression it is "satisfying," enjoyable. In this sense, Art is in itself a "happy end"; despair becomes sublime, pain beautiful.

The artistic presentation of the Crucifixion throughout the centuries is still the best example for this aesthetic transfiguration. Nietzsche saw in the Cross "the most subterranean conspiracy of all times—a conspiracy against sanity, beauty, health, courage, spirit, nobility of the soul, a conspiracy *against life itself*" (*The Antichrist 62*). The Cross as aesthetic object denounces the repressive force in the beauty and spirit of Art: "a conspiracy against life itself."

Nietzsche's formula may well serve to elucidate the impetus and the scope of today's rebellion against Art as part and parcel of the affirmative bourgeois culture—a rebellion sparked by the now intolerable, brutal conflict between the potential and the actual, between the very real possibilities of liberation and the indeed all but conspiratorial efforts, by the powers that be, to prevent this liberation. It seems that the aesthetic sublimation is approaching its historical limits, that the commitment of Art to the ideal, to the beautiful and the sublime, and with it the "holiday" function of Art, now offends the human condition. It also seems that the cognitive function of

Art can no longer obey the harmonizing "law of beauty": the contradiction between form and content shatters the traditional Form of Art.

The rebellion against the very Form of Art has a long history. At the height of classical aesthetics, it was an integral part of the romanticist program; its first desperate outcry was Georg Büchner's indictment that all idealistic Art displays a "disgraceful contempt for humanity." The protest continues in the renewed efforts to "save" Art by destroying the familiar, dominating forms of perception, the familiar appearance of the object, the thing because it is part of a false, mutilated experience. The development of Art to nonobjective art, minimal art, antiart was a way toward the liberation of the subject, preparing it for a new object-world instead of accepting and sublimating, beautifying the existing one, freeing mind and body for a new sensibility and sensitivity which can no longer tolerate a mutilated experience and a mutilated sensibility.

And then: the step to "living art" (a *contradictio in adjecto?*), Art in motion, *as* motion. In its own internal development, in its struggle against its own illusions, Art comes to join the struggle against the powers that be, mental and physical, the struggle against domination and repression—in other words, Art, by virtue of its own internal dynamic, is to become a *political force*. It refuses to be for the museum or mausoleum, for the exhibitions of a no longer existing aristocracy, for the holiday of the soul and the elevation of the masses; it wants to be *real*. Today Art enters the forces of rebellion only as it is desublimated: a living Form which gives word and image and sound to the unnameable, to the lie and its debunking, to the horror and to the liberation from it, to the body and its sensibility as the source and seat of all "aesthetics," as the seat of the soul and its culture, as the first "apperception" of the spirits, *Geist*:

Si l'on s'occupe de son corps, on a quelques chances de s'apercevoir qu'on possède aussi un esprit. *Je danse donc je suis!* [2]

[2] Maurice Béjart, quoted in *Nouvelle Observateur* (Paris), No. 223.

Living Art, antiart in all its variety—is its aim self-defeating? All these frenetic efforts to produce the absence of Form, to substitute the real for the aesthetic object, to ridicule oneself and the bourgeois customer—are they not so many activities of frustration, already part of the entertainment industry and the museum culture? I believe the aim of the "new art" is self-defeating because it retains, and must retain, no matter how "minimally," the Form of Art as different from nonart, and it is the Art-Form itself which frustrates the intention to reduce or even annul this difference, to make Art "real," "living."

Art cannot become reality, cannot realize itself without cancelling itself as Art in *all* its forms, even in its most destructive, most minimal, most "living" forms. The gap which separates Art from reality, the essential otherness of Art, its "illusory" character, can be reduced only to the degree to which *reality itself* tends toward Art as reality's own Form, that is to say, in the course of a revolution, with the emergence of a free society. In this process the artist would participate—as *artist* rather than as political *activist*. For the tradition of Art cannot be simply left behind or discarded; that which it has achieved, shown, and revealed in authentic forms contains a truth *beyond* immediate realization or solution, perhaps beyond any realization and solution.

The antiart of today is condemned to remain Art, no matter how "anti" it strives to be. Incapable of bridging the gap between Art and reality, of escaping from the fetters of the Art-Form, the rebellion against "form" only succeeds in a loss of artistic quality: illusory destruction, illusory overcoming of alienation. The authentic *œuvres,* the true avant-garde of our time, far from obscuring this distance, far from playing down alienation, *enlarge* it and harden their incompatibility with the given reality to an extent that defies any (behavioral) application. They fulfill in this way the cognitive function of Art (which is its inherent radical, "political" function), that is, to name the unnameable, to confront man with the dreams he betrays and the crimes he forgets. The greater the terrible con-

132)   HERBERT MARCUSE

flict between that which is and that which can be, the more will
the work of art be estranged from the immediacy of real life,
thought, and behavior—even political thought and behavior.
I believe that the authentic avant-garde of today are not those
who try desperately to produce the absence of Form and the
union with real life, but rather those who do not recoil from
the exigencies of Form, who find the new word, image, and
sound which are capable of "comprehending" reality as only
Art can comprehend—and negate it. This authentic new Form
has emerged in the work (already "classic") of Schönberg,
Berg, and Webern; of Kafka and Joyce; of Picasso; it continues today in such achievements as Stockhausen's *Spirale*
and Samuel Beckett's novels. They invalidate the notion of the
"end of art."

In contrast, the "living art," and especially the "living
theater" of today, does away with the Form of estrangement:
in eliminating the distance between the actors, the audience,
and the "outside," it establishes a familiarity and identification
with the actors and their message which quickly draws the
negation, the rebellion into the daily universe, as an enjoyable
and understandable element of this universe. The participation
of the audience is spurious and the result of previous arrangements; the change in consciousness and behavior is itself part
of the play—illusion is strengthened rather than destroyed.

There is a statement by Marx: "These petrified [social] conditions must be forced to dance by singing to them their own
melody." Dance will bring the dead world to life and make it
a human world. But today "their own melody" seems no longer
communicable except in forms of extreme estrangement and
dissociation from all immediacy—in the most conscious and
deliberate forms of Art.

I believe that "living art," the "realization" of Art can only
be the work of a qualitatively different society in which a new
type of men and women, no longer the subjects or objects of
exploitation, can develop, in their life and work, the vision of
the suppressed *aesthetic* possibilities of men and things—
aesthetic not as to the specific property of certain objects (the

objet d'art) but as forms and modes of existence corresponding to the reason and sensibility of free individuals (Marx: "the sensuous appropriation of the world"). The realization of Art, the "new art," is conceivable only as the process of constructing the universe of a free society—in other words: Art as a Form of reality.

Art as a Form of reality: it is impossible to ward off the horrible associations provoked by this notion, such as gigantic programs of beautification, artistic corporation offices, aesthetic factories, industrial parks. These associations belong to the practice of repression. "Art as a Form of reality" means not the beautification of the given, but the construction of an entirely different and opposed reality. The aesthetic vision is part of the *revolution*; it is a vision of Marx: "the animal constructs (*formiert*) only according to need; man forms also in accordance with the laws of beauty."

It is impossible to concretize Art as a Form of reality: it would then be creativity, a creation in the material as well as intellectual sense, a juncture of technique and the arts in the total reconstruction of the environment, a juncture of town and country, industry and nature after all have been freed from the horrors of commercial exploitation and beautification, so that Art can no longer serve as a stimulus of business. Evidently the very possibility of creating such an environment depends on the total transformation of the existing society: a new mode and new goals of production; a new type of human being as producer; the end of role-playing, of the established social division of labor, of work and pleasure.

Would such realization of Art imply the "invalidation" of the traditional arts? In other words, would it imply the "atrophy" of the capability to understand and enjoy them, atrophy of the intellectual faculty and the sensuous organs to experience the arts of the past? I suggest a negative answer. Art is transcendent in a sense which distinguishes and divorces it from any "daily" reality we can possibly envisage. No matter how free, society will be inflicted with necessity— the necessity of labor, of the fight against death and disease,

of scarcity. Thus the arts will retain forms of expression germane to them—and only to them: of a beauty and truth antagonistic to those of reality. There is, even in the most "impossible" verses of the traditional drama, even in the most impossible opera arias and duets, some element of rebellion which is
still "valid." There is in them some faithfulness to one's pas-
sions, some "freedom of expression" in defiance of common
sense, language, and behavior which indicts and contradicts
the established ways of life. It is by virtue of this "otherness"
that the beautiful in the traditional arts would retain its
truth. And this otherness could not and would not be canceled
by the social development. On the contrary: what would be
canceled is the *opposite:* namely, the false, conformist, and
comfortable reception (and creation!) of Art, its spurious
integration with the Establishment, its harmonization and
sublimation of repressive conditions. Then, perhaps for the
first time, men could *enjoy* the infinite sorrow of Beethoven
and Mahler because it is *aufgehoben* (overcome and preserved)
in the reality of freedom. And perhaps for the first time men
would *see* with the eyes of Corot, of Cézanne, of Monet because
the perception of these artists has helped to form this reality.